Polish for Beginners

A Comprehensive Guide for Learning the Polish Language Fast

Contents

Introduction

You are about to immerse yourself in the Polish language, and you won't be disappointed. This book will equip you with the basic knowledge and necessary language skills that will give you a real boost. You will have the chance to casually go through the Polish grammar basics without hard and daunting examination. Moreover, you will have the real chance to use your speaking skills throughout the whole book!

This book is not a textbook. You will, of course, be given some exercises, but they won't focus on the result. Here, the process is the most significant indicator of your fluency.

Before you start

The book consists of four chapters. First, you will start with the very basics and some simple exercises. Then, you will get familiar with Polish grammar. In the third chapter, you will have the opportunity to master your conversational skills. There will be many useful expressions and questions that may be vital during your trip to Poland. The last chapter contains essential vocabulary. After each part, you will also have a chance to revise all the words.

Are you ready? Good luck!

Chapter 1 – The Very Basics

The Polish Alphabet

If you have seen the Polish alphabet before, you would've noticed some weird letters, such as ą, ę, ó, ż, etc. However, there is nothing to worry about. The Polish alphabet is quite simple—since it shares many features with the English alphabet.

The Polish alphabet derives from the Latin alphabet, but the pronunciation has remained purely Slavic. Thus, Polish contains some unusual letters that you won't find in Western European alphabets. Moreover, Polish has some letter clusters that are called digraphs and trigraphs (you will see them later). Interestingly, letters x, v, and q are absent in Polish, even though they are common in Latin.

To start, take a close look at single letters and their pronunciation. You will notice an English word that contains a similar sound. Be careful! Some sounds (especially vowels) are not identical. The nearest equivalents are provided.

THE POLISH ALPHABET:

Polish letter/English sound/pronunciation example:

A a/u/as in fun

Ą ą/on, om/as in long

B b/b/as in bat

C c/ts/as in bits

Ć ć/ch/as in cheek

D d/d/as in dog

E e/e/as in red

Ę ę/en, em/as in dense

F f/f/as in frog

G g/g/as in gap

H h/ch/as in hamster (heavily enunciated)

I i/ee/as in cheek

J j/y/as in yeti

K k/c/as in call

L l/l/as in look

Ł ł/w/as in wall

M m/m/as in mom

N n/n/as in nose

Ń ń/ng (soft)/as in onion

O o/o/as in hot

Ó ó/u/as in push

P p/p/as in push

R r/r/as in Rome (rolled)

S s/s/as in seek

Ś ś/sh (soft)/as in sheep

T t/t/as in top

U u/u/as in push

W w/v/as in vital

Y y/y/as in rhythm

Z z/z/as in zebra

Ź ź/zh/as in Niger (very soft)

Ż ż/zh/as in pleasure (hard)

All in all, there are thirty-two single letters in the Polish alphabet. Before moving on to diphthongs that may cause some confusion, you need to practice the single sounds.

Exercise: Try to pronounce the Polish letters.

A a/u

Ą ą/on, om

B b/b

C c/ts

Ć ć/ch

D d/d

E e/e

Ę ę/en, em

F f/f

G g/g

H h/ch

I i/ee

J j/y

K k/c

Ll/l

Ł ł/w

M m/m

N n/n

Ń ń/ng

O o/o

Ó ó/u

P p/p

R r/r

S s/s

Ś ś/sh

T t/t

U u/u

W w/v

Y y/y

Z z/z

Ź ź/zh

Ż ż/zh

Congrats! You have managed to pronounce the Polish alphabet, although you've most likely faced some problems with the letters that are absent in English. That is fine. You need to train your articulatory muscles to move differently. The more you practice, the easier the pronunciation will become.

Now, take a closer look at some weird clusters, the so-called Polish diphthongs and triphthongs—these may be the hardest to grasp. You are about to really exercise your jaw and tongue.

POLISH DIPHTHONGS

Polish diphthong/English sound/pronunciation example:

Ch/ch/as in hamster

Ci/ch/as in cheek

Cz/ch/as in chalk

Dz/dz/as in goods (but with voiced s)

Dzi/dz/as in duke (very soft)

Dź/dz/as in duke (very soft)

Ni/ni/as in onion

Rz/s/as in treasure

Si/sh/as in sheep (soft)

Sz/sh/as in shark (hard)

Szcz/shch/- this is a consonant cluster that is absent in English; however, you try to join the sounds/sh/as in shark and/ch/as in chalk -/shch /

Zi/zh /as in Niger (very soft)

That was probably tough, with the *szcz* the hardest one because there is no such letter combination in the English language. The best way to start learning Polish is to get acquainted with the Polish sounds. There will be many hissing sounds coming from your mouth as you practice the Polish diphthongs. Essentially, Polish is considered a language of snakes!

Exercise: Try to pronounce Polish diphthongs.

Ch/ch

Ci/ch

Cz/ch

Dz/dz

Dzi/dz

Dź/dz

Ni/ni

Rz/s

Si/sh

Sz/sh

Szcz/shch

Zi/zh

Good job! You will quickly become a master of Polish sounds. Just a little more practice and you will get there.

Now it is time to discuss some interesting aspects of the Polish alphabet. As you have probably noticed, there is a significant difference between English and Polish, as far as alphabets are concerned. English sounds can be represented by multiple letter combinations, whereas Polish is simpler here. For example, the English sound [i] can be represented in the script in many ways (e, ee, i, y, and so on). In Polish, however, the sound [i] is represented only by the letter i. So, if you keep practicing, you will eventually get used to Polish sounds. Polish sounds may seem tough at the beginning, yet the journey becomes easier and easier with time.

There is one more thing that you should be aware of—the Polish orthography. There are some sounds in Polish that have different written representations. Although there aren't many of them, you need to, at least, know that they exist to avoid confusion in the future.

POLISH ORTOGRAPHY

[The sound] – Written representation 1/Written representation 2

[u] – u/ó

[h] (heavily aspirated) – h/ch

[zh] (hard) – ż/rz

[zh] (soft) – ź/zi

[sh] (soft) – ś/si

[ch] (soft) – ć/ci

[ng] (soft) – ń/ni

[om] – ą/om

With this Polish orthography, you don't have to practice it too hard. The best way to learn it is to get familiar with it by reading texts and seeing the words. If you make a mistake, don't worry—even Polish people struggle with the orthography since you have to learn it by heart. Remember why you want to learn Polish—you want to communicate, not produce perfect pieces of text!

Numbers

Although the rules of creating Polish numbers are quite simple, the pronunciation of Polish numbers can be tricky since you have to deal with the hardest sounds. That is why you will need to put in some effort and practice. For now, take a look at the smallest numbers—the ones from 0 to 10.

0 – zero

1 – jeden

2 – dwa

3 – trzy

4 – cztery

5 – pięć

6 – sześć

7 – siedem

8 – osiem

9 – dziewięć

10 – dziesięć

Have you seen those new letters? English speakers face many problems with the pronunciation of Polish numbers. Thus, you need to stay here for a little longer and practice.

Exercise: Repeat the Polish numbers.

zero – zero

one – jeden

two – dwa

three – trzy

four – cztery

five – pięć

six – sześć

seven – siedem

eight – osiem

nine – dziewięć

ten – dziesięć

Very good! Now try to repeat all the numbers one by one.

zero

zero, jeden

zero, jeden, dwa

zero, jeden, dwa, trzy

zero, jeden, dwa, trzy, cztery

zero, jeden, dwa, trzy, cztery, pięć

zero, jeden, dwa, trzy, cztery, pięć, sześć

zero, jeden, dwa, trzy, cztery, pięć, sześć, siedem

zero, jeden, dwa, trzy, cztery, pięć, sześć, siedem, osiem

zero, jeden, dwa, trzy, cztery, pięć, sześć, siedem, osiem, dziewięć

zero, jeden, dwa, trzy, cztery, pięć, sześć, siedem, osiem, dziewięć, dziesięć

Good job! You have just counted to ten! Now it is time to expand your horizons and take a look at numbers from 11 to 19:

11– jedenaście

12 – dwanaście

13 – trzynaście

14 – **czter**naście

15 – **pięt**naście

16 – **szes**naście

17 – siedemnaście

18 – osiemnaście

19 – **dziewięt**naście

You don't have to learn these numbers by heart. All you need to do is discover some patterns and try to follow them. Look at the numbers from 11 to 19 again. Have you noticed some regularities?

The Polish *–naście* is an equivalent of the English *–teen*. If you want to make, for example, *seventeen*, you take *seven* and add *–teen*. The Polish rule is the same—you take the number from 0 to 9 and add *–naście*. But be careful! There are some numbers like *czternaście, piętnaście, szesnaście,* or *dziewiętnaście* that require slight changes.

That was pretty easy. Now it is time to polish your pronunciation.

Exercise: Repeat Polish numbers from 11 to 19.

11 – jedenaście

12 – dwanaście

13 – trzynaście

14 – **czter**naście

15 – **pięt**naście

16 – **szes**naście

17 – siedemnaście

18 – osiemnaście

19 – **dziewię**tnaście

Very good! You are making huge progress! But you won't stop here. There are more numbers.

20 – **dwa**dzieścia

30 – **trzy**dzieści

40 – **czter**dzieści

50 – **pięć**dziesiąt

60 – **sześć**dziesiąt

70 – **siedem**dziesiąt

80 – **osiem**dziesiąt

90 – **dziewięć**dziesiąt

100 – sto

You have just learned some bigger Polish numbers. Now, it is time to practice. You definitely need to say *dziewięćdziesiąt* accurately!

Exercise: Repeat the Polish numbers.

20 – **dwa**dzieścia

30 – **trzy**dzieści

40 – **czter**dzieści

50 – **pięć**dziesiąt

60 – **sześć**dziesiąt

70 – **siedem**dziesiąt

80 – **osiem**dziesiąt

90 – **dziewięć**dziesiąt

100 – sto

Now that you know the *rounded* numbers, you need to learn the other ones. The pattern is simple: you just read what you see from left to right. Here are some examples.

21 – dwadzieścia jeden

55 – pięćdziesiąt pięć

48 – czterdzieści osiem

37 – trzydzieści siedem

92 – dziewięćdziesiąt dwa

75 – siedemdziesiąt pięć

In Polish, you don't write a dash in two-digit numbers—you just write what you see.

Exercise: Create the numbers in Polish.

24 –

27 –

36 –

41 –

49 –

54 –

69 –

73 –

82 –

99 –

100 –

Good job! You have officially learned Polish numbers!

Months and Days of the Week

If you have seen names of days and months in other languages like German or Spanish, you've probably noticed the similarities. However, when it comes to Polish, you need to almost start from scratch.

Months:

Styczeń – January

Luty – February

Marzec – March

Kwiecień – April

Maj – May

Czerwiec – June

Lipiec – July

Sierpień – August

Wrzesień – September

Październik – October

Listopad – November

Grudzień – December

Since these are some new names, you need to memorize them quickly.

Exercise: Repeat the Polish months.

Styczeń

Styczeń, luty

Styczeń, luty, marzec

Styczeń, luty, marzec, kwiecień

Styczeń, luty, marzec, kwiecień, maj

Styczeń, luty, marzec, kwiecień, maj, czerwiec

Styczeń, luty, marzec, kwiecień, maj, czerwiec, lipiec

Styczeń, luty, marzec, kwiecień, maj, czerwiec, lipiec, sierpień

Styczeń, luty, marzec, kwiecień, maj, czerwiec, lipiec, sierpień, wrzesień

Styczeń, luty, marzec, kwiecień, maj, czerwiec, lipiec, sierpień, wrzesień, październik

Styczeń, luty, marzec, kwiecień, maj, czerwiec, lipiec, sierpień, wrzesień, październik, listopad

Styczeń, luty, marzec, kwiecień, maj, czerwiec, lipiec, sierpień, wrzesień, październik, listopad, grudzień

The months are significantly different since Polish is a Slavic language and English is a Germanic language. If you look at other Slavic languages, you will probably notice some similar names of months.

Days of the week:

Poniedziałek – Monday

Wtorek – Tuesday

Środa – Wednesday

Czwartek – Thursday

Piątek – Friday

Sobota – Saturday

Niedziela – Sunday

Nothing is probably familiar to you regarding the above either. That is why you need to practice and memorize the names. If you forget something, just go through the list again and again. Eventually, you will become a pro!

Exercise: Repeat the Polish days of the week.

Poniedziałek

Wtorek

Środa

Czwartek

Piątek

Sobota

Niedziela

Well done! Now, here is a bonus skill. If you want to say *today is…*, you need to use:

Dziś jest…

Repeat one more time: **Dziś jest…**

Bonus exercise: Try to say the following phrases in Polish.

Today is Monday.

Today is Tuesday.

Today is Wednesday.

Today is Thursday.

Today is Friday.

Today is Saturday.

Today is Sunday.

Very good! You are getting better and better. When it comes to reading or writing the date in Polish, it usually starts with a day and ends with a year. You have to use a numeral, not a number, if you read the date (similar to the English pattern). However, Polish numerals are quite tough for a beginner learner since they need to be declined by gender, number, and case. So, for now, just stop here and take a look at the seasons.

Seasons:

Wiosna – Spring

Lato – Summer

Jesień – Autumn/Fall

Zima – Winter

Well done! If you don't remember much, just go back to the exercises and go through the vocabulary lists multiple times. You are not at school; therefore, you're not in a hurry. If you feel confident enough, you can go straight to the next part!

Nouns

Since Polish and English do not share many similarities in terms of grammar, you need to, at least, be aware of some basic differences, starting with the nouns.

English nouns are quite simple. If there is one, you don't change anything. If there's two or more, you just add –s at the end (with a few exceptions), and that is basically it. When it comes to Polish, though, the story gets more complicated. Polish nouns have to be declined by gender, number, and case. While number and gender declensions are quite understandable concepts for an English learner, the cases tend to scare learners.

Cases:

There are seven cases in total. Polish nouns change the ending, depending on which case they are declined. And that is all you should know for now, as declensions at this point are unnecessary. Mastering the rules will not make your learning efficient. Even if you apply a wrong ending, your message will be understood anyway. So, now take a look at some examples to see how nouns work in different Polish cases.

A BOOK – KSIĄŻKA

Nominative – książka

Genitive – książki

Dative – książce

Accusative – książkę

Ablative – (z) książką

Locative – (o) książce

Vocative – książko!

A COMPUTER – KOMPUTER

Nominative – komputer

Genitive – komputera

Dative – komputerowi

Accusative – komputer

Ablative – (z) komputerem

Locative – (o) komputerze

Vocative – komputerze!

As you have probably noticed, the endings are quite different. There is no point in making you remember the rules. Your learning has to be quick, efficient, and fun! The best way is to learn the cases gradually, in context, and by using associations. If you try to learn all variations of the same word by heart, you will find yourself overwhelmed sooner or later. So, don't worry.

Even some proper names have to be declined by case. Look at the examples below:

Francja [France] – feminine noun

Nominative – Francja

Genitive – Francji

Dative – Francji

Accusative – Francję

Ablative – (z) Francją

Locative – (o) Francji

Vocative – Francjo!

Włochy [Italy] – plural noun

Nominative – Włochy

Genitive – Włoch

Dative – Włochom

Accusative – Włochy

Ablative – (z) Włochami

Locative – (o) Włoszech

Vocative – Włochy!

If you are starting to panic, take a deep breath. This theoretical part is included here only to give you an idea of how the language works and in what ways it is different from your mother tongue. Don't expect any advanced grammar in later exercises—just have fun!

Number:

As mentioned, cases are just a part of the bigger picture, so now look at how the grammatical number works in Polish.

Singular and plural are formed with different endings that correspond with gender. English plural involves the ending -s with only a few exceptions, whereas Polish plural involves endings such as -y, -i, -e, or -a.

In the Polish plural form, there are only two genders—masculine and non-masculine. There aren't any rules to apply in terms of using plural and singular. Here are some examples:

English translation/Polish Singular/Polish Plural

A house/dom/domy

A wallet/portfel/portfele

An umbrella/parasolka/parasolki

A book/książka/książki

A computer/komputer/komputery

A girl/dziewczyna/dziewczyny

A boy/chłopak/chłopaki

A dog/pies/psy

A cat/kot/koty

The best way to learn the rules is to see them in context and memorize. If you try to follow the rules, you will quickly get lost and lose your communicative fluency.

Gender:

Polish grammatical gender is way different from the English one since Polish masculine, feminine, and neuter do not correspond with the actual sex. Using feminine or masculine gender while talking about objects is the standard in Polish. For instance, the Polish word *banan* [banana] is masculine, the word *truskawka* [strawberry] is feminine, and the word *mango* [mango] is neutral.

To sum up what you have learned here:

1. Polish is quite complicated in terms of grammar. At least, it differs significantly from English.

2. Polish grammatical number is irregular and requires adding different endings, depending on factors like gender, etc.

3. Polish gender does not correspond with the actual sex. Even inanimate objects can be masculine or feminine.

4. There are seven cases in Polish that require different endings. There are so many of them that learning the rules would be completely useless.

5. You don't have to learn the declensions. Just be aware of the key differences to be more confident in the future.

Articles

The three basic articles in English are *a, an,* and *the.* In contrast, the Polish language does not have any articles. You most likely don't think much about using articles in English, as you produce them naturally. It is something you have heard and seen since childhood. From the native Polish speaker's perspective, though, the idea of English articles is hard to grasp. Despite knowing the rules and exceptions, even advanced and proficient Polish speakers of English cannot fully understand English articles.

Fortunately, you do not have to learn any articles since Polish doesn't contain any. So, take a break and relax for a little while.

Pronouns

There are only a few personal pronouns in English. Can you remember all of them? What are they? You probably remember that there are only three versions of a personal pronoun in English. For example, *me*, *my,* and *mine* or *you*, *your,* and *yours*.

Unfortunately, Polish pronouns have more versions than English ones. They act like nouns, so they need to be declined by gender, number, and case. Each pronoun looks different in each case, gender, and number, so that is why there are so many of them.

Ja – I

Ty – you

On – he

Ona – she

Ono – it

My – we

Wy – you

Oni/one – they

Those are the basic versions of pronouns. They are in the nominative case, which means that they are in the primary form. They are the same as the English ones. Repeat them.

Ja – I

Ty – you

On – he

Ona – she

Ono – it

My – we

Wy – you

Oni/one – they

During the repetition, you probably noticed two different versions of the pronoun *they*. The first one is masculine, and the second one is feminine. When you refer to a group of men or a mixed group, you need to use *oni*. You have to use one when you refer to a group of women. So, the pronoun *oni* is more popular since it can serve both as a reference to a mixed group or a group of men. You can't use *one*, even though the group consists of one man and ten women. Now, practice the pronouns again.

Exercise: Try to guess the Polish pronouns based on the English equivalents.

I

You

He

She

It

We

You

They

Try to do the same exercise once again, but in random order.

You

She

They

I

He

You

It

We

Well done! You have learned Polish pronouns. It is a huge step towards building the simplest sentences. Remember about the distinction between a masculine *oni* and a feminine *one*.

Presently, this book won't teach you about the rest of the pronouns that appear in different cases. It would not give any positive results. You would get confused and quickly lose your motivation. So, it is time to move on to the next topic—provided you are confident enough with the pronouns. If you need more practice, do it now and come back later.

Adjectives

Not only do nouns introduce the mess in Polish, but the adjectives are also quite messy. In fact, they need to stay in compliance with gender, number, and case, so they too require different endings. To make things less complicated, they don't act like separate random words—they depend directly on the noun they describe. So, if the noun is singular feminine in the dative case, the adjective will also be singular feminine in the dative case.

Below, you will see how the adjectives work in different cases, genders, and numbers. Be aware that you don't have to memorize the declensions—they are only here to show you how Polish works. You definitely need to learn adjectives in context, provided that you are more or less familiar with the patterns. Look at the adjective *mały*, which means *small*:

mały samochód – a small car (masculine noun, singular)

[Nominative] mały samochód

[Genitive] małego samochodu

[Dative] – małemu samochodowi

[Accusative] – mały samochód

[Ablative] – (z) małym samochodem

[Locative] – (o) małym samochodzie

[Vocative] – mały samochodzie!

mała dziewczynka – a small girl (feminine noun, singular)

[Nominative] mała dziewczynka

[Genitive] małej dziewczynki

[Dative] – małej dziewczynce

[Accusative] – małą dziewczynkę

[Ablative] – (z) małą dziewczynką

[Locative] – (o) małej dziewczynce

[Vocative] – mała dziewczynko!

małe dziecko – a small child (neutral noun, singular)

[Nominative] małe dziecko

[Genitive] małego dziecka

[Dative] – małemu dziecku

[Accusative] – małe dziecko

[Ablative] – (z) małym dzieckiem

[Locative] – (o) małym dziecku

[Vocative] – małe dziecko!

małe samochody – small cars (masculine noun, plural)

[Nominative] małe samochody

[Genitive] małych samochodów

[Dative] – małym samochodom

[Accusative] – małe samochody

[Ablative] – (z) małymi samochodami

[Locative] – (o) małych samochodach

[Vocative] – małe samochody!

małe dzieci – small children (non-masculine noun, plural)

[Nominative] małe dzieci

[Genitive] małych dzieci

[Dative] – małym dzieciom

[Accusative] – małe dzieci

[Ablative] – (z) małymi dziećmi

[Locative] – (o) małych dzieciach

[Vocative] – małe dzieci!

Those declensions were quite complicated, but you know how they work, and it is a huge step towards mastering the Polish language.

Now it is time to look at the adjectives in terms of gradation. The good news is that Polish gradation works nearly the same as the English one. Short adjectives require an ending, and longer adjectives require a word before them. Of course, there are a few exceptions. For now, just take a look at the short adjectives, and go through all of the adjectives multiple times to learn them automatically.

Długi (long) – dłuższy (longer) – najdłuższy (the longest)

Krótki (short) – krótszy (shorter) – najkrótszy (the shortest)

Niski (low) – niższy (lower) – najniższy (the lowest)

Chudy (skinny) – chudszy (skinnier) – najchudszy (the skinniest)

Ciepły (warm) – cieplejszy (warmer) – najcieplejszy (the warmest)

Zimny (cold) – zimniejszy (colder) – najzimniejszy (the coldest)

Jasny (light) – jaśniejszy (lighter) – najjaśniejszy (the lightest)

Ciemny (dark) – ciemniejszy (darker) – najciemniejszy (the darkest)

Miły (nice) – milszy (nicer) – najmilszy (the nicest)

Szczęśliwy (happy) – szczęśliwszy (happier) – najszczęśliwszy (the happiest)

Smutny (sad) – smutniejszy (sadder) – najsmutniejszy (the saddest)

Młody (young) – młodszy (younger) – najmłodszy (the youngest)

Stary (old) – starszy (older) – najstarszy (the oldest)

Nowy (new) – nowszy (newer) – najnowszy (the newest)

Śmieszny (funny) – śmieszniejszy (funnier) – najśmieszniejszy (the funniest)

Fajny (cool) – fajniejszy (cooler) – najfajniejszy (the coolest)

Gruby (fat) – grubszy (fatter) – najgrubszy (the fattest)

Ciężki (heavy) – cięższy (heavier) – najcięższy (the heaviest)

Silny (strong) – silniejszy (stronger) – najsilniejszy (the strongest)

Słaby (weak) – słabszy (weaker) – najsłabszy (the weakest)

Późny (late) – późniejszy (later) – najpóźniejszy (the latest)

Wczesny (early) – wcześniejszy (earlier) – najwcześniejszy (the earliest)

Twardy (hard) – twardszy (harder) – najtwardszy (the hardest)

Miękki (soft) – miększy (softer) – najmiększy (the softest)

Tani (cheap) – tańszy (cheaper) – najtańszy (the cheapest)

Biały (white) – bielszy (whiter) – najbielszy (the whitest)

Mądry (smart) – mądrzejszy (smarter) – najmądrzejszy (the smartest)

You probably noticed the pattern. Comparative adjectives require the ending *–szy*. To complicate matters, the main part of the adjective changes a bit too. When you want to create a superlative adjective, you have to add *naj-* at the beginning of the comparative adjective. There are some adjectives in Polish that act like short adjectives, but their English equivalents act like long adjectives:

Drogi (expensive) – droższy (more expensive) – najdroższy (the most expensive)

Piękny (beautiful) – piękniejszy (more beautiful) – najpiękniejszy (the most beautiful)

Ważny (important) – ważniejszy (more important) – najważniejszy (the most important)

There is a second way of grading adjectives, the so-called descriptive gradation. In English, you just add *more* and *the most*, while in Polish, you need to add *bardziej* and *najbardziej*. Take a look at some examples:

Inteligentny (intelligent) – bardziej inteligentny (more intelligent) – najbardziej inteligentny (the most intelligent)

Popularny (popular) – bardziej popularny (more popular) – najbardziej popularny (the most popular)

Zielony (green) – bardziej zielony (greener) – najbardziej zielony (the greenest)

This gradation is way simpler. Interestingly, some adjectives can be graded both in a descriptive and non-descriptive way:

Inteligentny (intelligent) – bardziej inteligentny (more intelligent) – najbardziej inteligentny (the most intelligent)

Inteligentny – inteligentniejszy – najinteligentniejszy

Popularny (popular) – popularniejszy (more popular) – najpopularniejszy (the most popular)

Popularny – bardziej popularny – najbardziej popularny

Zielony (green) – bardziej zielony (greener) – najbardziej zielony (the greenest)

Zielony – zieleńszy – najzieleńszy

Of course, there are some exceptions, just as in English. Here are the most common ones:

Dobry (good) – lepszy (better) – najlepszy (the best)

Zły (bad) – gorszy (worse) – najgorszy (the worst)

Duży (big) – większy (bigger) – największy (the biggest)

Mały (small) – mniejszy (smaller) – najmniejszy (the smallest)

Wysoki (tall) – wyższy (taller) – najwyższy (the tallest)

Chapter 2 – Grammar Bits

Before you start learning some useful Polish words and expressions, you need to familiarize yourself with some basic grammatical concepts. To acquire the core of the language quickly and efficiently, you have to know the theoretical foundations of the target language. You won't have to memorize declensions and other difficult material—you will just go through the most important concepts you need to be aware of.

Verbs – how do they work?

Polish verbs, as like the nouns, are highly complicated. It is because Polish verbs require eleven different patterns of conjugation. Keep in mind that the eleven patterns are applicable only in the present tenses. The past tense requires the other pattern. Do not try learning them by heart—it would not be beneficial. Instead, this book provides some tips and learning hacks that can improve and speed up your learning.

In order not to get lost, you need to find some similarities and patterns. Polish verbs in an infinitive form (the form without a person) end with [-ć]. If you decline the verb by all the grammatical persons, you will notice that the ending changes accordingly. Look at three different Polish verbs: *robić* [to do], *czytać* [to read] and *śpiewać* [to sing].

To do – robić

I do – ja robię

You do – ty robi**sz**

He does – on robi

She does – ona robi

It does – ono robi

We do – my robi**my**

You do – wy robi**cie**

They do – oni/one robi**ą**

To read – czytać

I read – ja czyta**m**

You read – ty czyta**sz**

He reads – on czyta

She reads – ona czyta

It reads – ono czyta

We read – my czyta**my**

You read – wy czyta**cie**

They read – oni/one czyta**ją**

To sing – śpiewać

I sing – ja śpiewa**m**

You sing – ty śpiewa**sz**

He sings – on śpiewa

She sings – ona śpiewa

It sings – ono śpiewa

We sing – my śpiewa**my**

You sing – wy śpiewa**cie**

They sing – oni/one śpiewa**ją**

Did you notice the pattern? Go through the list once again and look carefully at the endings. You will probably guess the rules on your own.

Despite the abundance of declension patterns, Polish verbs are rather regular. You just need to observe them carefully and you will become confident enough. So, what about the above verbs? Despite some slight changes, the pattern stays the same:

> •in the first person *ja,* there is always the ending [-m] or [-ę];
>
> •in the second person *ty*, there is always the ending [-sz];
>
> •in the third person *on/ona/ono,* there is nearly always no ending—you just delete [-ć] from the original infinitive form;
>
> •in the first person plural, there is almost always the ending [-my];
>
> •in the second person plural, there is almost always the ending [-cie]; and
>
> •in the third person plural, there is always the ending [-ą].

The rules can be applied to nearly all Polish verbs. Of course, there are some exceptions, but you don't have to know them now. However, you need to be aware of the fact that some verbs undergo some changes in the main part. For instance, the substitution of a letter, the addition of a new letter, or the deletion of a letter. These changes are there for a reason. Without them, the pronunciation (which is tough already) would be really hard, even for Polish people who are natural-born "snakes".

Don't get discouraged if you confuse some letters—you will probably be understood anyway. The more you immerse yourself in the new language, the more automatic your use will be.

Exercise: Try to conjugate *grać* [to play]. Take your time and apply the endings analogically, based on the examples that you have been shown.

TIP: The verb *grać* is similar to *czytać*.

To play – grać

I play –

You play –

He plays –

She plays –

It plays –

We play –

You play –

They play –

Here are the answers:

I play – ja gram

You play – ty grasz

He plays – on gra

She plays – ona gra

It plays – ono gra

We play – my gramy

You play – wy gracie

They play – oni/one grają

Good! Hopefully, you understand the pattern.

Exercise: Try to conjugate *dzwonić* [to call]. Take your time and apply the endings analogically, based on the examples that you have been shown.

TIP: The verb *dzwonić* is similar to *robić*.

To call – dzwonić

I call –

You call –

He calls –

She calls –

It calls –

We call –

You call–

They call–

Here are the answers:

To call – dzwonić

I call – ja dzwonię

You call – ty dzwonisz

He calls – on dzwoni

She calls – ona dzwoni

It calls – ono dzwoni

We call – my dzwonimy

You call – wy dzwonicie

They call – oni/one dzwonią

Excellent! You have just learned how not to get lost in the sea of Polish grammar! That is a huge step towards fluency in conversation.

Basic Polish verbs

You are about to learn the most important and useful Polish verbs that will give your fluency a boost! Of course, there are no shortcuts like in the previous part—you need to learn all these verbs by heart. Fortunately, you will learn them in the context of a sentence. Of course, you don't have to memorize all the sentences—they are here to show you the situation in which the verb can be used. It is a pretty long list, so take your time and go through it at least three times. You can go back to it every day. Good luck!

Być – to be (Jestem Paula. – I am Paula.)

Mieć – to have (Mam kota. – I have a cat)

Iść – to go (Idę do sklepu. – I'm going to the store.)

Robić – to do/to make (Robię zakupy. – I'm doing shopping.)

Próbować – to try (Próbowałem wiele razy. – I've tried many times.)

Pomagać – to help (Pomagam tacie. – I'm helping my dad.)

Grać/bawić się – to play (Lubię bawić się na dworze. – I like playing outside.)

Spacerować – to walk (Lubisz spacerować? – Do you like walking?)

Uczyć się – to learn (W szkole muszę się uczyć. – I have to learn at school.)

Mieszkać – to live (Mieszkam w mieście. – I live in a city.)

Pracować – to work (Pracuję w dużej firmie. – I work in a big company.)

Jeść – to eat (Chodźmy coś zjeść! – Let's go eat something!)

Pić – to drink (Ona wypiła już kawę. – She has already drunk her coffee.)

Pisać – to write (Piszę e-mail. – I'm writing an e-mail.)

Czytać – to read (On czyta książkę. – He's reading a book.)

Liczyć – to count (Mogę na ciebie liczyć? – Can I count on you?)

Rysować – to draw (Uczę się rysować. – I'm learning how to draw.)

Malować – to paint (Oni malują. – They're painting.)

Widzieć – to see (Nie widzę go. – I can't see him.)

Wyglądać/spoglądać – to look (Dobrze wyglądasz! – You look good!)

Oglądać – to watch (Oglądam telewizję – I'm watching TV.)

Słyszeć – to hear (Usłyszałem dziwny głos. – I've just heard a strange voice.)

Słuchać – to listen (Słuchamy muzyki. – We're listening to music.)

Spać – to sleep (Idę spać. – I'm going to sleep.)

Gotować – to cook (Umiesz gotować? – Can you cook?)

Sprzątać – to clean (Muszę dzisiaj sprzątać mieszkanie. – I have to clean the flat today.)

Podróżować – to travel (Podrózuję do Chin. – I'm traveling to China.)

Jechać – to drive (Jadę do domu. – I'm driving home.)

Latać – to fly (Chciałbyś polecieć do Londynu? – Would you like to fly to London?)

Pływać – to swim (Nie umiem pływać. – I can't swim.)

Biegać – to run (Ona teraz biega. – She's running now.)

Siedzieć – to sit (Usiądźcie. – Sit down.)

Rozpoczynać – to begin (Przedstawienie zaczyna się o 8:00. – The show begins at 8 AM.)

Stać – to stand (Stań tutaj. – Stand here.)

Kłaść – to put (Gdzie mogę położyć tę paczkę? – Where can I put this parcel?)

Wychodzić – to leave (Właśnie wychodziliśmy. – We were just leaving.)

Przychodzić – to come (Przyjdź do mojego biura o 9:00. – Come to my office at 9 AM.)

Śpiewać – to sing (Nie umiem śpiewać. – I can't sing.)

Tańczyć – to dance (Zatańczymy? – Shall we dance?)

Pamiętać – to remember (Pamiętaj o mnie. – Remember about me.)

Zapominać – to forget (Zapomniałem o spotkaniu! – I've just forgotten about the meeting!)

Wybierać – to choose (Wybierz jedną opcję. – Choose one option.)

Zamykać – to close (Zamknij drzwi, proszę. – Close the door, please.)

Otwierać – to open (Czy mógłbyś otworzyć okno? – Could you open the window?)

Tworzyć – to create (Stwórzmy własny projekt! – Let's create our own project!)

Budować – to build (On buduje dom. – He's building a house.)

Pokazywać/przedstawiać – to show (Pokażesz mi? – Can you show me?)

Czuć – to feel (Czuję się dobrze. – I feel good.)

Czuć/wąchać – to smell (Czuję coś dziwnego. – I'm smelling something strange.)

Smakować/próbować – to taste (Spróbuj tej zupy. – Taste this soup.)

Myśleć – to think (Myślę, że… – I think that…)

Rosnąć – to grow (Dzieci rosną bardzo szybko. – Children grow very fast.)

Myć – to wash (Muszę umyć samochód. – I need to wash my car.)

Wierzyć – to believe (Wierzę, że… – I believe that…)

Mówić – to speak (Mów głośniej! – Speak up!)

Powiedzieć – to say (Powiedz coś! – Say something!)

Rozmawiać – to talk (Możemy teraz porozmawiać? – Can we talk now?)

Dawać – to give (Czy mógłbyś mi to dać? – Could you give me this?)

Brać – to take (Muszę wziąć dzień wolnego. – I have to take a day off.)

Pożyczać – to borrow (Pożyczysz mi swój samochód? – Could you borrow me your car?)

Pożyczać – to lend (Pożyczę ci mój samochód. – I will borrow you my car.)

Skakać – to jump (On skacze bardzo wysoko. – He's jumping very high.)

Odejść – to quit (Odchodzę! – I quit!)

Uderzyć – to hit (Mocno mnie uderzyła! – She hit me hard!)

Strzelać – to shoot (Strzelaj! – Shoot!)

Kupować – to buy (Chcę kupić nowy samochód. – I want to buy a new car.)

Sprzedawać – to sell (Muszę sprzedać dom. – I have to sell my house.)

Wymieniać – to exchange (Czy mogę wymienić pieniądze? – Can I exchange my money?)

Wygrywać – to win (Moja drużyna wygrała zawody! – My team won the competition!)

Przegrywać – to lose (Moja drużyna przegrała zawody – My team lost the competition.)

Rozumieć – to understand (Rozumiesz? – Do you understand?)

Uczyć – to teach (Uczę w szkole podstawowej. – I teach at primary school.)

Łapać – to catch (Łap piłkę! – Catch the ball!)

Well done! You have learned the most important Polish verbs. Before you start a new part, check how many verbs you remember:

To read –

To do –

To buy –

To sell –

To learn –

To borrow –

To win –

To talk –

To watch –

To choose –

To open –

To build –

To swim –

To write –

To exchange –

To show –

To smell –

To run –

To give –

Very good! You are a pro!

Modal Verbs

These are verbs that require using another verb in an infinitive form (a form without a person). Can you think of any modal verbs in English? Just look at the first word in the previous sentence, and you will find the first English modal verb! Here are the English modal verbs:

I **can** do it.

I **must** do it.

I **should** do it.

Can you see the pattern? As previously mentioned, modal verbs require using a different verb. Polish modal verbs act similarly. They just require another verb that is in its infinitive form. Here are some examples:

Mogę to zrobić.

Muszę to zrobić.

Powinienem to zrobić.

There are two main differences. Firstly, the Polish word order is quite free, so sometimes the sentences will look slightly different from the English translations. Nevertheless, the pattern is the same—you just need a modal verb and a second verb in the infinitive form. Secondly, you need to conjugate the modal verb according to the person, gender, and number.

Can – móc

I can – ja mogę

You can – ty możesz

He can – on może

She can – ona może

It can – ono może

We can – my możemy

You can – wy możecie

They can – oni/one mogą

Must – musieć

I must – ja muszę

You must – ty musisz

He must – on musi

She must – ona musi

It must – ono musi

We must – my musimy

You must – wy musicie

They must – oni/one muszą

That is it! Modal verbs are not that scary, but you need to remember to conjugate them.

Reflexive verbs

You have basically acquired the essence of Polish verbs. However, there is one more group of Polish verbs that you need to know. They are called *reflexive verbs*. You can easily find such verbs in English. These are the ones that require adding a reflexive pronoun like *yourself/myself/themselves*, etc. Can you think of an example of an English reflexive verb? Think for a moment.

You have probably found many examples. English reflexive verbs require the pronoun that changes according to the person. For example, you say *I wash myself*, but you have to say *she washes herself*, *we wash ourselves*, and so on. In Polish, however, the situation is very simple. Instead of using a pronoun after the verb, you just add the word *się*, and that is basically it. Isn't it simple? If only the rest of Polish grammar was that simple… Here are some examples:

To wash oneself – myć się

I wash myself – ja myję się

You wash yourself – ty myjesz się

He washes himself – on myje się

She washes herself – ona myje się

It washes itself – ono myje się

We wash ourselves – my myjemy się

You wash yourselves – wy myjecie się

They wash themselves – oni/one myją się

To help oneself – częstować się

I help myself – ja częstuję się

You help yourself – ty częstujesz się

He helps himself – on częstuje się

She helps herself – ona częstuje się

It helps itself – ono częstuje się

We help ourselves – my częstujemy się

You help yourselves – wy częstujecie się

They help themselves – oni/one częstują się

Now, it is time to practice!

Exercise: Try to conjugate *kąpać się* (meaning similar to *myć się* [to wash oneself]). There will be some slight changes in spelling, but don't get discouraged if you make a mistake—you are here to learn how to add the reflexive pronoun.

To wash oneself – kąpać się

I wash myself –

You wash yourself –

He washes himself –

She washes herself –

It washes itself –

We wash ourselves –

You wash yourselves –

They wash themselves –

The answers:

To wash oneself – kąpać się

I wash myself – kąpię się

You wash yourself – kąpiesz się

He washes himself – kąpie się

She washes herself – kąpie się

It washes itself – kąpie się

We wash ourselves – kąpiemy się

You wash yourselves – kąpiecie się

They wash themselves – kąpią się

Congrats! You have made huge progress.

Tenses

You have learned Polish verbs! Well done! Yet you probably know that verbs can be expressed in different tenses—past, present, and future. In English, many grammatical tenses are used to express different contexts. In Polish, however, there are only three tenses—past, present, and future. What is more, the Polish verbs have two different aspects.

You need to know that the whole concept of Polish tenses is rather different from what you know from your mother tongue. Just look carefully at some examples to see how Polish tenses work.

In Polish, you can use the same structure to express different situations:

Myję zęby każdego dnia. – <u>I brush</u> my teeth every day.

<u>Myję zęby</u> teraz. – <u>I am brushing</u> my teeth now.

<u>Myję</u> zęby od siedmiu lat. – <u>I have brushed</u> my teeth for seven years.

<u>Myję</u> zęby od siedmiu lat – <u>I have been brushing</u> my teeth for seven years.

<u>Robię</u> zadania domowe w weekendy. – <u>I do</u> my homework on weekends.

<u>Robię</u> zadania domowe. – <u>I am doing</u> my homework.

<u>Robię</u> zadania domowe odkąd poszedłem do szkoły – <u>I have been doing</u> my homework since I went to school.

<u>Robię</u> zadania domowe odkąd poszedłem do szkoły – <u>I have done</u> my homework since I went to school.

Polish does not have the continuous and perfect aspect. The concepts can be expressed similarly. The same pattern applies to the past, yet the verb has to be in the past form:

Zrobiłem/zrobiłam zadanie domowe wczoraj. – *I did* my homework yesterday.

Robiłem/robiłam zadanie domowe kiedy zadzwonił telefon. – *I was doing* my homework when the telephone rang.

Zrobiłem/zrobiłam właśnie zadanie domowe. – *I have just done* my homework.

Nie wiedziałem/wiedziałam czemu dostałem 1, ponieważ *zrobiłem/zrobiłam* zadanie domowe. – I didn't know why I got an E because I *had done* my homework.

Now look at some future forms:

Zrobię zadanie domowe. – *I will do* my homework.

Zrobię zadanie domowe zanim mama przyjedzie. – *I will have done* my homework by the time my mom comes back.

To sum up, Polish is different from English in terms of tenses. It is not a huge difference, but you need to be aware of it to avoid confusion in the future. This book won't give you more complicated metalinguistic explanations since you don't need any. Just focus on the basics and try to learn some useful things!

Quiz

Before moving on to chapter three, which is all about conversations in Polish, here is a short quiz. A quick revision always helps to remember more!

Exercise 1 – Try to conjugate the verbs based on the tips that you have been given.

To do – robić

I do

You do

He does

She does

It does

We do

You do

They do

To read – czytać

I read

You read

He reads

She reads

It reads

We read

You read

They read

Exercise 2 – Try to conjugate the reflexive verb.

To help oneself – częstować się

I help myself –

You help yourself –

He helps himself –

It helps itself –

We help ourselves –

You help yourselves –

They help themselves –

Exercise 3 – Guess the meaning of the verbs provided.

To run –

To give –

To take –

To jump –

To dance –

To leave –

To put –

To understand –

To hit –

To shoot –

To sit –

To begin –

To create –

Exercise 4 – Try to conjugate modal verbs:

Can – móc

I can –

You can –

He can –

She can –

It can –

We can –

You can –

They can –

Must – musieć

I must –

You must –

He must –

She must –

It must –

We must –

You must –

They must –

Chapter 3 – Let's Talk

Congratulations! You have managed to go through the first two chapters, which introduced you to the foundations of the Polish language. Now it is time to put your knowledge into practice! This chapter mainly focuses on communication. You will learn how to have a basic conversation in Polish, how to order a meal, how to ask for directions, and much more!

Greetings

In this part, you will learn how to say hi to friends, your boss, or some strangers on the street.

Polish people have a set of greetings similar to the English ones with one main exception—there is no *good afternoon*. Instead, Polish people use a more general expression that can be literally translated as *good day*:

Dzień dobry! – Good morning/Good afternoon!

Repeat:

Dzień dobry! – Good morning/Good afternoon!

Dzień dobry is used for morning and afternoons, yet when it gets dark, Polish people use:

Dobry wieczór! – Good evening!

Repeat it twice:

Dobry wieczór! – Good evening!

Dobry wieczór! – Good evening!

If you want your greeting to be extremely formal, you can add something like *Mr./Mrs.* or *Ms.* and the name of the person you want to greet:

Dzień dobry Pani ... – Good morning Mrs./Ms. ...

Dzień dobry Panie ... – Good morning Mr. ...

And now repeat the expression and add a name of your choice to it:

Dzień dobry Pani ... – Good morning Mrs./Ms. ...

Dzień dobry Panie ... – Good morning Mr. ...

You can also formalize your dobry wieczór. Just add *Pani/Panie* and the name of your choice:

Dobry wieczór Pani ... – Good evening Mrs./Ms. ...

Dobry wieczór Panie ... – Good evening Mr. ...

Now repeat the expressions with names:

Dobry wieczór Pani ... – Good evening Mrs./Ms. ...

Dobry wieczór Panie ... – Good evening Mr. ...

These were some formal greetings. Of course, Polish people have some informal greetings too! The most common one is:

Cześć! – Hello/Hi!

At this point, you might have problems with the pronunciation. So to repeat your cześć at least five times. Remove your foreign accent once and for all!

Cześć!

Cześć!

Cześć!

Cześć!

Cześć!

Before you start saying *cześć* to everyone, you need to know one more thing. The Polish *cześć* differs from the English *hi/hello* in terms of use. Don't say *cześć* to address an older person you don't know (even a waiter or a shop assistant). When you are at work or school, always say *dzień dobry* to your boss, supervisor, or teacher. Even lecturers at a university always greet their students with *dzień dobry*! What is more, teachers say *dzień dobry* when they enter a classroom full of small kids. Generally, even if you have known the teacher for a while, you have to say *dzień dobry*.

Polish people use cześć to say goodbye. So, cześć is a really universal word.

Cześć! – Bye!

Remember, Cześć is rather informal, so if you want to say goodbye to your teacher/boss, etc., you have to use:

Do widzenia! – Goodbye!

Repeat it four times to acquire the sound at the end:

Do widzenia! – Goodbye!

Do widzenia! – Goodbye!

Do widzenia! – Goodbye!

Do widzenia! – Goodbye!

Of course, if you want a highly formal expression, you can add Pani/Panie + a name.

Do widzenia Pani … – Goodbye Mrs./Ms. …

Do widzenia Panie ... – Goodbye Mr. ...

Repeat the expressions twice:

Do widzenia Pani ... – Goodbye Mrs./Ms. ...

Do widzenia Panie ... – Goodbye Mr. ...

Do widzenia Pani ... – Goodbye Mrs./Ms. ...

Do widzenia Panie ... – Goodbye Mr. ...

After you say your dzień dobry or cześć, you need to proceed with the conversation. English people always use stuff like how do you do?/how are you? Polish people have similar expressions, yet you need to be careful with them (which is explained in a moment).

Co tam?/Co u ciebie? – How are you?/How do you do?

Repeat the expressions:

Co tam?/Co u ciebie? – How are you?/How do you do?

Co tam?/Co u ciebie? – How are you?/How do you do?

When you ask a Polish person *co tam/co tam u ciebie,* do not expect an answer like *fine, good,* etc. A Polish person will usually start to talk about his/her life in general (school, work, family, important events). So, the Polish *co tam* usually starts a conversation about life, whereas the English *how are you* is a natural follow-up after *hi/hello.*

You have just learned how to start a conversation! Now, it is time to practice!

Exercise: Try to greet different Polish people. Use a suitable greeting.

Greet your teacher

Greet your mom

Greet your friend

Greet your lecturer

Greet a shop assistant that is older than you

Greet your uncle

Greet a waiter in a restaurant

Greet your coworker

Greet your boss

Exercise: Say goodbye in Polish to:

Your parents

Your teacher

Your waiter at a restaurant

Your friend

A shop assistant

Your boss

Very good! You should be getting more and more confident. Before you finish the topic of greetings, here are some colloquial greetings that are used mainly by Polish teenagers and young adults:

Siema! – Hey!

Elo! – Yo! (a very informal form of addressing your close friends)

Jak leci? – What's up?

Trzymaj się! – Take care!

Na razie! – Bye!

Dzięki! – Thanks!

Spoko!/Ok!/Okej! – Ok!/No problem! (Polish people say *ok* very often)

Repeat:

Siema! – Hey!

Elo! – Yo!

Jak leci? – What's up?

Trzymaj się! – Take care!

Na razie! – Bye!

Dzięki! – Thanks!

Spoko!/Ok!/Okej! – Ok!/No problem!

Introducing Yourself

You have already learned how to greet different people, so it is time to introduce yourself. Did you know that there are many ways of introducing yourself in Polish?

The most common way of saying your name in Polish is just saying your name. It is the most natural way of introducing yourself. If you want to get more sophisticated, you can say *jestem,* which means *I am.* Easy, right?

Exercise: Try to introduce yourself in Polish now.

Jestem + your name

The second way is even more sophisticated. Here you need to say *mam na imię...* which means *my name is...* Good! Don't forget to add your name!

Exercise: Try to introduce yourself in Polish using *mam na imię* now.

Now try the most formal way of introducing yourself in Polish! Remember: this way is used only during some formal events. If you want to introduce yourself formally, you need to say *nazywam się +* your full name [first name and surname]; for example, *Nazywam się Tomasz Kowalski.*

Exercise: Try to introduce yourself in Polish using *nazywam się* now.

You have just learned how to introduce yourself in Polish. Don't forget that the most common informal way is simply saying your name, and stick with this version while taking part in a casual conversation. You can't sound artificial. When it comes to some formal situations like business lunches, etc., it is better to introduce yourself with phrases like *jestem, mam na imię,* or *nazywam się.*

Exercise: Try to introduce yourself in different ways.

You have learned how to introduce yourself, yet you need to know how to ask somebody about his/her name. At least you need to understand the question to be able to introduce yourself.

There are two main ways of asking this question. You can say a phrase *jak masz na imię,* which means *what is your name?* If you ask this question, the person will always say only their first name. Try asking this question now.

Exercise: Ask the person what his/her name is in Polish.

The second, more formal way is using the phrase *jak się nazywasz?* If you say this phrase, the person will probably say his/her full name. In other words, you can expect something like *nazywam się* + full name.

Exercise: Ask the person what his/her name is in Polish (in a formal way).

It is time to introduce yourself again! When you hear *jak masz na imię?* you can say *jestem* + your name or *mam na imię* + your name. When you hear *jak się nazywasz?* you usually say *nazywam się* + your full name. Make these phrases work in practice:

Exercise: Try to answer in Polish to some questions.

Jak masz na imię?

Jak się nazywasz?

Jak masz na imię?

Jak się nazywasz?

Hopefully, you can clearly see the difference. Remember that you do not have to say these phrases when introducing yourself. You can just say your name, and it will be fine!

Stop here for a moment and summarize what you have already learned. You can introduce yourself, ask a person about his/her name, and successfully reply to the question as well. However, you need to keep going since the conversation can't end after some short introduction.

A person has just asked you about your name, and you replied. Now it is time to ask the question. Using the same phrase would sound artificial, so you can simply say *a ty?* which means *and you?*

Exercise: Try to introduce yourself and ask someone to introduce himself/herself.

However, you have not finished yet! Go back to some formal stuff. Remember how to ask a person about his/her full name? You need to say *jak się nazywasz*? If you don't know someone at a formal event, you need to use a phrase like

Jak się Pan/Pani nazywa? – What is your name? (formal)

Very good! You have learned all the ways of introducing yourself in Polish. Now it is time to gather all these different ways together and use them in some context. You are about to ask different people about their names, yet you need to remember about using formal and informal patterns.

Exercise: Try to ask about a person's name based on the provided context:

A new person in your class

Your father's friend from school

Your new teacher

Your new boss

A random person you've just met in a restaurant

A new member of your sports team

A new coworker

A policeman

Casual talk

So, the conversation is progressing, and you need to be able to ask some additional questions. Greeting someone and introducing yourself is a good beginning, yet you need to say more than that. This book will teach you different expressions and questions that will give you the foundations of Polish conversation. In this part, you will learn how to ask a person about age, nationality, place of living, language, and opinion!

You will start with a question about age. In Polish, it sounds like this:

Ile masz lat?

Repeat this question three times:

Ile masz lat?

Ile masz lat?

Ile masz lat?

Now it is time to say how old you are. There are two ways of telling your age. You can simply tell the number, or you can use the phrase:

Mam... lat.

Even though the phrase can be translated into English as *I'm... years old*, you can probably see the difference. Polish people do not use the verb *być* [to be] while telling the age. Instead, they use *mieć* [to have]. A literal translation would be *I have... years*. Before you start the exercise, go back to the part about numbers because you will need them in a moment. If you remember them, you can start the exercise now.

Exercise: Try to tell in Polish how old you are using different numbers.

I am 18 years old.

I am 54 years old.

I am 33 years old.

I am 97 years old.

I am 6 years old.

I am 45 years old.

I am 23 years old.

Now tell your age.

However, there is a formal way of asking a person about the age. You need to use the pronouns *Pan/Pani/Państwo.*

Ile ma Pan/Pani lat?

Ile mają Panie/Panowie/Państwo lat?

Repeat:

Ile ma Pan/Pani lat?

Ile mają Panie/Panowie/Państwo lat?

Exercise: Ask about someone's age politely based on the context provided.

A woman

A man

A group of women

A group of men

A group of men and women

Language

Imagine that you have just entered a foreign country. The first question you will probably ask is one about language. This is the most common introductory question in a foreign conversation. If you don't feel confident enough to have a conversation in Polish, you will be able at least to say that you don't speak the language. If you want to ask someone if he/she speaks a particular language, you need to say:

Mówisz po angielsku? – Do you speak English?

Mówisz po polsku? – Do you speak Polish?

And now look at the formal ways:

Czy mówi Pan po angielsku? (one male)

Czy mówi Pani po angielsku? (one female)

Czy mówią Panie po angielsku? (two or more females)

Czy mówią Panowie po angielsku? (two or more males)

Czy mówią Państwo po angielsku? (two or more males and females)

Czy mówi Pan po polsku? (one male)

Czy mówi Pani po polsku? (one female)

Czy mówią Panie po polsku? (two or more females)

Czy mówią Panowie po polsku? (two or more males)

Czy mówią Państwo po polsku? (two or more males and females)

It is better to use formal forms if you don't know the person and he/she is older than you. Polish people use formal questions quite frequently.

Now it is time to tell someone that you speak/don't speak Polish/English.

If you want to say that you **speak** Polish/English, you need to use:

Mówię po angielsku. – I speak English.

Mowię po polsku. – I speak Polish.

Repeat:

Mówię po angielsku. – I speak English.

Mowię po polsku. – I speak Polish.

If you want to say that you **don't speak** Polish/English, you need to use:

Nie mówię po angielsku. – I don't speak English.

Nie mówię po polsku. – I don't speak Polish.

If you want to say that you **don't speak** Polish/English **very well**, you need to use:

Nie mówię dobrze po angielsku. – I don't speak English very well.

Nie mówię dobrze po polsku. – I don't speak Polish very well.

Exercise: Try to say the following phrases in Polish:

Do you speak English? (informal way)

Do you speak Polish? (male, formal way)

Do you speak English? (female, formal way)

Do you speak Polish? (males, formal way)

Do you speak English? (females, formal way)

Do you speak Polish? (males and females, formal way)

I speak Polish.

I speak English.

I don't speak Polish.

I don't speak English.

I don't speak Polish very well.

I don't speak English very well.

Very good! You have just learned one of the most useful phrases.

Nationality and place of living

In this part, you will learn how to ask a person about his/her nationality, place of living, and address. Start from a broad context.

If you want to ask a person about his/her nationality, you need to say:

Skąd pochodzisz? – Where are you from?

If you want to be polite, you need to say:

Skąd Pan/Pani pochodzi?

Skąd Panowie/Panie/Państwo pochodzą?

If you want to tell someone where you are from, you need to say:

Pochodzę z ... – I am from ...

Exercise: Try to ask the questions and say the phrases in Polish.

Where are you from?

Where are you from? (polite, male)

Where are you from? (polite, female)

Where are you from? (polite, males)

Where are you from? (polite, females)

Where are you from? (polite, males and females)

I come from ...

Now you will learn how to ask a person about his/her place of living. If you want to do that, you need to say:

Gdzie mieszkasz? – Where do you live?

If you want to keep the formal style, you need to use the following phrases:

Gdzie Pan/Pani mieszka? – Where do you live? (one male/one female)

Gdzie Panie/Panowie/Państwo mieszkają? – Where do you live? (females/males/males and females)

If you want to tell someone where you live, you need to use the following phrase:

Mieszkam w/na... (city/region etc.) – I live in...

Exercise: Try to say the following phrases in Polish:

Where do you live?

Where do you live? (male)

Where do you live? (female)

Where do you live? (males)

Where do you live? (females)

Where do you live? (males and females)

If you want to ask someone about his/her address, you just simply ask:

Jak jest twój adres? – What is your address?

If you want to keep the formal style, you have to ask the following questions:

Jaki jest Pana adres?

Jaki jest Pani adres?

Jaki jest Państwa adres?

If you want to reply, you just simply say your address. It is the most common way used both in formal and informal styles.

You have just learned another ingredient of an initial conversation! In the next part, you will learn more advanced questions and phrases. However, before you start...

Exercise: Try to say the following phrases in Polish:

Where are you from?

Where are you from? (polite, male)

Where are you from? (polite, female)

Where are you from? (polite, males)

Where are you from? (polite, females)

Where are you from? (polite, males and females)

I come from …

Where do you live?

Where do you live? (male)

Where do you live? (female)

Where do you live? (males)

Where do you live? (females)

Where do you live? (males and females)

Jak jest twój adres?

Jaki jest Pana adres?

Jaki jest Pani adres?

Jaki jest Państwa adres?

Opinion

You have already learned some introductory questions and phrases that can help you start your conversation in Polish. This is the last part that will teach you the basic Polish conversation. After this subchapter, you will take part in some real situations that can happen during a trip to Poland. Here you will learn how to express your opinion (likes/dislikes) and how to ask a person about his/her opinion on a particular thing or activity. It is a very useful conversational skill since it can help you proceed with the conversation and avoid uncomfortable silences due to limited language skills.

You can ask someone about his/her likes/dislikes in many ways, but you will start with the simple way. In Polish, it looks like this:

Co lubisz? – What do you like?

Co lubisz najbardziej? – What do you like the most?

A formal version looks like this:

Co Pan/Pani lubi (najbardziej)? – What do you like (the most)?

Co Panie/Panowie/Państwo lubią (najbardziej)? – What do you like (the most)?

If you want to share your opinion, you can say:

Lubię... – I like...

Najbardziej lubię... – I like... the most.

Nie lubię... – I don't like...

Najbardziej nie lubię... – I don't like... the most

You can use the Polish *lubię/nie lubię* to express an opinion on activities, too. However, these questions are constructed differently when compared to English. See how they work.

Try to say that you like *ciasto* [a cake].

Lubię ciasto.

Now, try to say that you don't like cake.

Nie lubię ciasta.

Have you noticed the difference? In the second phrase, *ciasto* changed into *ciasta*. Why? Because the phrase nie lubię [I don't like] requires using a different case of the noun. Polish cases are really complicated and you don't need to learn them at the beginning of your language journey. Just keep in mind that they exist somewhere. Even if you say *nie lubię ciasto* (which is incorrect), your message will be understood anyway—you will just sound foreign.

Now, try to say that you like playing football.

Lubię grać w piłkę nożną.

Now you don't like playing football:

Nie lubię grać w piłkę nożną.

Here nothing has changed. When talking about activities, the Polish *lubię/nie lubię* phrases always require an infinitive form of a verb. So, the literal translation into English would look like this: *I like to play football/I don't like to play football.*

Exercise: Try to say the following phrases in Polish.

I like cake.

I don't like cake.

I like to play football.

I don't like to play football.

You have just learned the basics of Polish conversation. Now it is time for a longer exercise—you need to join all the elements together and practice them for a little while.

Exercise: Try to say the following phrases in Polish.

Hi!

Good morning!

Good evening!

Good morning, Mr….

Good evening, Mrs…

How are you?

Bye!

Goodbye, Mr…

Goodbye, Mrs…

Do you speak English?

Do you speak Polish?

Do you speak English? (formal)

Do you speak Polish? (formal)

Where do you live?

I live in…

Where are you from?

I am from…

What is your name?

What is your name? (formal, male)

What is your name? (formal, female)

I am…

My name is…

My name is (formal + full name)

How old are you?

How old are you? (formal, male)

How old are you? (formal, female)

I am 23 years old.

I am 45 years old.

I am 19 years old.

I am 56 years old.

What is your address?

What is your address? (formal, male)

What is your address? (formal, female)

What is your address? (formal, male and female)

I like cake.

I don't like cake.

I like to play football.

I don't like to play football.

What do you like?

What do you like the most?

What do you like? (formal, male)

What do you like? (formal, female)

That was a long exercise, but hopefully, you nailed it! As stated, it is time to move on to some real-life situations. In the following subchapters, you will be introduced to some dialogues that may happen in a restaurant, at a hotel or a bar. After familiarizing yourself with the dialogue, you will have a chance to practice and use your language skills.

In the restaurant

Before you start practicing real conversations, there are a couple of things you need to know about the organization of the lessons you are about to take part in. Each lesson will contain some dialogues. The first dialogue will be in Polish with an English translation. The second dialogue will be the same but without the English translations. After getting familiarized with the dialogues, you will have the chance to do some interactive exercises.

When it comes to vocabulary, go to the last chapter of the book since it contains the most useful vocabulary from each topic. You will find some extra words that you may find useful, especially at the beginning of your language journey.

Some dialogues will be more difficult than others, but don't get discouraged. Go through them multiple times, and you will gradually become more fluent in Polish.

When you visit a foreign country, you want to try its cuisine. You need to remember that some restaurants in Poland don't offer service in English. Of course, the most popular ones that are located in big cities will definitely hire waiters that speak fluent English. However, if you decide to spend some time in the countryside and go to a local restaurant, you might get surprised. That is why you need to be able to talk to your waiter in Polish!

DIALOGUE 1:

Dzień dobry! **Chciałbym/chciałabym** zamówić stolik dla dwóch osób. – Hello, I'd like to book a table for two people.

Dzień dobry, oczywiście. Na którą godzinę? – Hello, of course. What time?

Na osiemnastą. – 6 PM.

Ok. Czy mogę prosić o nazwisko? – Ok. Can I have your last name, please?

Oczywiście, Nowak. – Sure, Nowak.

Dziękuję bardzo i do zobaczenia. – Thank you and goodbye.

Do zobaczenia. – Goodbye.

That was the first dialogue! If you missed something, go through the dialogue once again. If you are a female, you need to say *chciałabym* instead of *chciałbym* at the beginning.

DIALOG 1 (WITHOUT TRANSLATIONS):

Dzień dobry! **Chciałbym/chciałabym** zamówić stolik dla dwóch osób.

Dzień dobry, oczywiście. Na którą godzinę?

Na osiemnastą.

Ok. Czy mogę prosić o nazwisko?

Oczywiście, Nowak.

Dziękuję bardzo i do zobaczenia.

Do zobaczenia.

Now it is time to do a quick exercise. Your lines have been removed from the dialogue, and you will have to say them!

EXERCISE 1:

Dzień dobry, oczywiście. Na którą godzinę?

Ok. Czy mogę prosić o nazwisko?

Dziękuję bardzo i do zobaczenia.

Now go through the dialogue once again and change the time and the number of people. Don't forget to say your real surname.

EXERCISE 2:

Dzień dobry, oczywiście. Na którą godzinę?

Ok. Czy mogę prosić o nazwisko?

Dziękuję bardzo i do zobaczenia.

Now it is time to order your first meal and something to drink!

DIALOGUE 2:

Dzień dobry! Czy mogę przyjąć zamówienie? – Hello! Can I take your order?

Tak, chciałbym/chciałabym zamówić pierogi. – Yes, I would like to order pierogi.

Oczywiście. Czy coś do picia? – Sure, something to drink?

Tak, poproszę kawę. – Yes. Coffee, please.

Czy coś jeszcze? – Anything else?

Nie, dziękuję. To wszystko na tę chwilę. – No, thanks. That's all for now.

DIALOGUE 2 (WITHOUT TRANSLATIONS):

Dzień dobry! Czy mogę przyjąć zamówienie?

Tak, chciałbym/chciałabym zamówić pierogi.

Oczywiście. Czy coś do picia?

Tak, poproszę kawę.

Czy coś jeszcze?

Nie, dziękuje. To wszytko na tę chwilę.

Do you remember the dialogue? Keep in mind that you need to use *chciałabym* instead of *chciałbym* if you are female. Are you ready for some interaction?

EXERCISE 1:

Dzień dobry! Czy mogę przyjąć zamówienie?

Oczywiście. Czy coś do picia?

Czy coś jeszcze?

Now talk to your waiter once again but order something different.

EXERCISE 2:

Dzień dobry! Czy mogę przyjąć zamówienie?

Oczywiście. Czy coś do picia?

Czy coś jeszcze?

Before you leave the restaurant, you need to pay, of course. You need to remember that Polish service differs from the English one. Usually, your waiter won't be coming to you every ten minutes. Sometimes you need to tell your waiter that you want to pay and leave the restaurant.

DIALOG 3:

Chciałbym/chciałabym zapłacić. – I'd like to pay.

Oczywiście. To będzie trzydzieści złotych. – Of course. That will be 30 zlotych.

Czy mogę zapłacić kartą? – Can I pay with credit card?

Niestety, tylko gotówką. – Only cash here, sorry.

Nie ma problemu. Proszę. – No problem. Here you are.

Dziękuję bardzo. Czy smakował posiłek? – Thank you very much. Did you enjoy the meal?

Tak. Był bardzo pyszny! Dziękuję. – Yes. It was delicious. Thanks.

Dziękujemy i zapraszamy ponownie. – Thank you and see you next time.

Do widzenia. – Goodbye.

DIALOGUE 3 (WITHOUT TRANSLATIONS):

Chciałbym/chciałabym zapłacić.

Oczywiście. To będzie trzydzieści złotych.

Czy mogę zapłacić kartą?

Niestety, tylko gotówką.

Nie ma problemu. Proszę.

Dziękuję bardzo. Czy smakował posiłek?

Tak. Był bardzo pyszny! Dziękuję.

Dziękujemy i zapraszamy ponownie.

Do widzenia.

That was quite long, but hopefully, you remembered everything.

EXERCISE 1:

Oczywiście. To będzie trzydzieści złotych.

Niestety, tylko gotówką.

Dziękuję bardzo. Czy smakował posiłek?

Dziękujemy i zapraszamy ponownie.

You have just learned how to survive in a Polish restaurant! You can book a table, order a meal, and pay! If you are not confident enough, you can go back to the dialogues and practice them multiple times. If you did great, you can move on to the next part.

At the airport

Polish airports are quite small compared to English or American ones. Even though the staff speaks fluent English, itis better to know some Polish phrases to avoid misunderstandings in some situations.

DIALOGUE 1:

Dzień dobry. Czy mogę zobaczyć Pana/Pani paszport? – Hello, may I see your passport, please?

Oczywiście, proszę. – Sure, here you are.

Dziękuję. Proszę położyć walizkę tutaj. – Thanks. Please put your luggage here.

Oczywiście. – Of course.

Proszę, oto Pana/Pani paszport. Miłego lotu. – Here is your passport. Have a nice flight.

Dziękuję bardzo. – Thank you very much.

So you have just registered your baggage. It is time to practice the dialogue without translations.

DIALOGUE 2 (WITHOUT TRANSLATIONS):

Dzień dobry. Czy mogę zobaczyć Pana/Pani paszport?

Oczywiście, proszę.

Dziękuję. Proszę położyć walizkę tutaj.

Oczywiście.

Proszę, oto Pana/Pani paszport. Miłego lotu.

Dziękuję bardzo.

EXERCISE 1:

Dzień dobry. Czy mogę zobaczyć Pana/Pani paszport?

Dziękuję. Proszę położyć walizkę tutaj.

Proszę, oto Pana/Pani paszport. Miłego lotu.

Your baggage is registered. If you got lost and you want to add some questions at the airport, here is a list of the most common expressions that may be helpful at the Polish airport. Go through them slowly and carefully. Focus on the pronunciation:

Przepraszam, gdzie jest strefa wolnocłowa? – Excuse me, where is the duty-free zone?

Przepraszam, gdzie jest hala odlotów? – Excuse me, where is the departure lounge?

Zgubiłem/Zgubiłam mój bagaż. – I've lost my luggage.

Czy mogę to zabrać jako bagaż podręczny? – Can I take this along as hand luggage?

Przykro mi, nie może Pan/Pani tego zabrać. – I'm sorry, you can't take this.

Chcę zabrać swój bagaż. – I want to take my luggage.

Proszę zapiąć pasy bezpieczeństwa. – Please, fasten your seat belts.

Prosimy nie zostawiać bagażu bez nadzoru. – Please, don't leave your luggage unattended.

Now repeat the phrases once again:

Przepraszam, gdzie jest strefa wolnocłowa?

Przepraszam, gdzie jest hala odlotów?

Zgubiłem/Zgubiłam mój bagaż.

Czy mogę to zabrać jako bagaż podręczny?

Przykro mi, nie może Pan/Pani tego zabrać.

Chcę zabrać swój bagaż.

Proszę zapiąć pasy bezpieczeństwa.

Prosimy nie zostawiać bagażu bez nadzoru.

Exercise: Say the phrases in Polish.

Ask where the duty-free zone is.

Ask where the departure lounge is.

Say that you want to take your luggage.

Ask whether you can take your bag as hand luggage.

Say that you lost your luggage.

Good job! You can go to any Polish airport, and you won't get lost!

At the train/bus station

You have just left the airport, and you probably want to get to your accommodation. The best way to do this is to take a bus or a train, especially when you decide to stay in a big city. When it comes to trains, you just go to the ticket office located inside the railway station and buy a ticket.

DIALOGUE 1:

Dzień dobry. Chciałbym kupić bilet do Warszawy. – Hello, I'd like to buy a ticket to Warsaw.

Oczywiście. Normalny czy ulgowy? – Sure. Normal or reduced?

Czy są zniżki dla studentów? – Are there any discounts for students?

Tak. Bilet studencki jest tańszy o połowę. – Yes. Student ticket is reduced to half price.

Ok. Poproszę jeden bilet studencki. – Ok. One student ticket, please.

Proszę bardzo. To będzie 10 złotych. – Of course. That will be 10 zlotych.

Czy mogę zapłacić kartą? – Can I pay with credit card?

Tak, oczywiście. – Yes, of course.

Dziękuję i do widzenia. – Thank you, and goodbye.

Do widzenia. – Bye.

Repeat the dialogue without translations.

DIALOG 1 (WITHOUT TRANSLATIONS):

Dzień dobry. Chciałbym kupić bilet do Warszawy.

Oczywiście. Normalny czy ulgowy?

Czy są zniżki dla studentów?

Tak. Bilet studencki jest tańszy o połowę.

Ok. Poproszę jeden bilet studencki.

Proszę bardzo. To będzie 10 złotych.

Czy mogę zapłacić kartą?

Tak, oczywiście.

Dziękuję i do widzenia.

Do widzenia.

EXERCISE 1:

Oczywiście. Normalny czy ulgowy?

Tak. Bilet studencki jest tańszy o połowę.

Proszę bardzo. To będzie 10 złotych.

Tak, oczywiście.

Do widzenia.

Excellent! Here are some extra phrases that might be useful if you decide to take the Polish train. Go through them carefully.

Czy mogę zobaczyć Pana/Pani bilet? – May I see your ticket, please?

Czy mogę zobaczyć Pana/Pani legitymację? – May I see your student ID, please?

Pociąg jest opóźniony. – The train is delayed.

Przepraszam, czy ten pociąg jedzie do Poznania? – Excuse me, does this train go to Poznań?

Przepraszam, o której odjeżdża pociąg do Wrocławia? – Excuse me, what time does the train to Wrocław leave?

Przepraszam, gdzie jest wagon sypialny? – Excuse me, where is the sleeping carriage?

Repeat these phrases a couple of times to learn them once and for all.

Czy mogę zobaczyć Pana/Pani bilet?

Czy mogę zobaczyć Pana/Pani legitymację?

Pociąg jest opóźniony.

Przepraszam, czy ten pociąg jedzie do Poznania?

Przepraszam, o której odjeżdża pociąg do Wrocławia?

Przepraszam, gdzie jest wagon sypialny?

Exercise: Try to say the phrases in Polish.

Ask the conductor where the sleeping carriage is.

Ask what time the train to Warsaw leaves.

Make sure that the train departs to Poznan.

Ask whether you can pay with a credit card.

Ask whether there are any discounts for students.

Buy two normal tickets.

Buy one reduced ticket.

You have just bought the tickets. Now, find your bus/train and enjoy your journey. Onward to the hotel!

At the hotel

Welcome to the hotel! The journey was quite exhausting, but you have finally reached your destination. It is time to go to the reception and get the key to your room.

DIALOGUE 1:

Dzień dobry. W czym mogę pomóc? – Hello, how can I help you?

Dzień dobry. Mam rezerwację dla dwóch osób. – Hello. I have a reservation for two people.

Czy mogę prosić o nazwisko? – May I have your last name, please?

Oczywiście. Nazywam się Lewandowski. – Sure. My last name is Lewandowski.

Ok. Oto Pana/Pani klucz. Pokój 308. – Ok. Here is your key. Room 308.

Dziękuję bardzo. O której godzinie jest śniadanie? – Thank you very much. What time is breakfast?

Śniadanie zaczyna się o godzinie ósmej, a kończy się o dziesiątej. – Breakfast starts at eight o'clock and finishes at ten o'clock.

Dziękuję. Gdzie jest restauracja? – Thanks. Where is the restaurant?

Restauracja jest tam. – The restaurant is right there.

Dziękuję bardzo. – Thank you!

Miłego dnia. – Have a nice day.

That dialogue was quite long. However, when you decide to stay at a hotel, you need to ask a couple of important questions. So, repeat the dialogue once again, without the translations.

DIALOG 1 (WITHOUT TRANSLATIONS):

Dzień dobry. W czym mogę pomóc?

Dzień dobry. Mam rezerwację dla dwóch osób.

Czy mogę prosić o nazwisko?

Oczywiście. Nazywam się Lewandowski.

Ok. Oto Pana/Pani klucz. Pokój 308.

Dziękuję bardzo. O której godzinie jest śniadanie?

Śniadanie zaczyna się o godzinie ósmej, a kończy się o dziesiątej.

Dziękuję. Gdzie jest restauracja?

Restauracja jest tam.

Dziękuję bardzo.

Miłego dnia.

Before you move on to the next topic, you need to be familiar with the most important phrases that might save your life at a Polish hotel. Sometimes things don't go as planned, and sometimes you just want to ask about a couple of things, so you need to know more than the dialogue you have just learned.

Czy mają Państwo jakieś wolne pokoje? – Do you have any rooms available?

Czy przyjmują Państwo również zwierzęta? – Are pets allowed?

Czy ręczniki i pościele są wliczone w cenę? – Are sheets and towels included?

O której godzinie jest obiadokolacja? – What time do you serve dinner?

Co jest w cenie zakwaterowania? – What's included in the cost of accommodation?

Czy w tym pokoju jest klimatyzacja? – Does this room have air-conditioning?

Klimatyzacja w moim pokoju nie działa. – The air-conditioning in my room is out of order.

Przepraszam, jakie jest hasło do Wi-Fi? – Excuse me, could you tell me the Wi-Fi password?

Chciałbym/Chciałabym dokonać rezerwacji. – I would like to make a reservation.

Proszę zostawić brudne ręczniki na podłodze. – Please, leave the dirty towels on the floor.

Chciałbym/chciałabym się wymeldować. – I would like to check-out, please.

Chciałbym /chciałabym dostać inny pokój. – I would like a different room.

Bardzo nam się podobało. – We really enjoyed our stay here.

These were the most important phrases. Since there were quite a lot of them, you need to repeat them a couple of times.

Czy mają Państwo jakieś wolne pokoje?

Czy przyjmują Państwo również zwierzęta?

Czy ręczniki i pościele są wliczone w cenę?

O której godzinie jest obiadokolacja?

Co jest w cenie zakwaterowania?

Czy w tym pokoju jest klimatyzacja?

Klimatyzacja w moim pokoju nie działa.

Przepraszam, jakie jest hasło do WiFi?

Chciałbym/Chciałabym dokonać rezerwacji.

Proszę zostawić brudne ręczniki na podłodze.

Chciałbym/chciałabym się wymeldować.

Chciałbym /chciałabym dostać inny pokój.

Bardzo nam się podobało.

Very good! You are getting better and better!

Exercise: Try to say the phrases in Polish.

Ask the receptionist whether there is any room available.

Say that you would like to check out.

Ask about the Wi-Fi password.

Ask the receptionist where the restaurant is.

Ask the receptionist what time breakfast is.

Ask the receptionist what time dinner is.

Ask the receptionist whether animals are allowed.

Ask the receptionist whether there is an air conditioner in your room.

Say that the air conditioner in your room isn't working.

Say to the receptionist that you enjoyed your stay.

Say to the receptionist that you have a reservation for two people.

Say your full name.

Well done! You will stay at a Polish hotel without any problems. You can pack your suitcases now!

Doing the shopping

So you have been staying in Poland for a couple of days. You've really enjoyed the country. You have visited some nice restaurants, traveled by trains and buses, and you've enjoyed your stay at a really nice hotel. It is time to do some shopping! Most of the Polish supermarkets don't require sophisticated spoken interaction since you only go to the checkout and pay. Nevertheless, here are some useful phrases that you may use in a supermarket.

IN THE SUPERMARKET:

Przepraszam, ile to kosztuje? – Excuse me, how much does it cost?

Czy chciałby Pan/chciałaby Pani zapłacić kartą czy gotówką? – Would you like to pay with cash or with a credit card?

Czy mogę prosić o paragon? – Can I have a receipt, please?

Proszę wprowadzić PIN. – Enter your PIN-code, please.

Dziś polecamy… – I recommend buying… today.

Ok, wezmę to. – Ok, I'll take it.

Przepraszam, gdzie znajdę owoce? – Excuse me, where can I find fruit?

Czy chciałby Pan/chciałaby pani torbę? – Would you like a plastic bag?

Ten produkt jest obecnie wyprzedany. – This item is currently out of stock.

Czy ten produkt jest w promocji? – Is this product on sale?

Chciałbym/Chciałabym zapłacić gotówką. – I would like to pay with cash.

Chciałbym/Chciałabym zapłacić kartą. – I would like to pay with a credit card.

Proszę, oto reszta. – Here's your change.

Czy jest Pan/Pani członkiem naszego klubu? – Are you a member of our loyalty program?

Revise the phrases as there are many of them.

Przepraszam, ile to kosztuje?

Czy chciałby Pan/chciałaby Pani zapłacić kartą czy gotówką?

Czy mogę prosić o paragon?

Proszę wprowadzić PIN.

Dziś polecamy…

Ok, wezmę to.

Przepraszam, gdzie znajdę owoce?

Czy chciałby Pan/chciałaby pani torbę?

Ten produkt jest obecnie wyprzedany.

Czy ten produkt jest w promocji?

Chciałbym/Chciałabym zapłacić gotówką.

Chciałbym/Chciałabym zapłacić kartą.

Proszę, oto reszta.

Czy jest Pan/Pani członkiem naszego klubu?

Exercise: Say the phrases in Polish.

Ask the cashier how much something costs.

Ask for a receipt.

Ask the shop assistant where you can find fruit.

Ask the shop assistant whether something is on sale.

Say that you would like to pay with cash.

Say that you would like to pay with a credit card.

Say that you don't want the bag.

Good job! You can go to the Polish supermarket. Now get some clothes!

IN A CLOTHES SHOP:

If you go to a Polish shopping center, you will probably notice shops like H&M, Zara, and many other popular ones. Here are the most useful phrases that might give you confidence when you decide to go to a clothing shop in Poland.

Dzień dobry, czy mogę to przymierzyć? – Hello, can I try this on?

Przepraszam, gdzie jest przymierzalnia? – Excuse me, where is the fitting room?

Chciałbym/chciałabym przymierzyć te buty. – I would like to try on these shoes.

Chciałbym/chciałabym zobaczyć tę bluzkę z wystawy. – I would like to see that shirt you have on display.

Noszę rozmiar 36. – I take a size 36.

Czy mógłby Pan/mogłaby Pani pomóc mi zapiąć ten zamek? – Could you help me with this zip?

Może to Pan/Pani zapakować to jako prezent? – Could you gift wrap it for me?

Czy są większe rozmiary? – Do you have it in a bigger size?

Czy są mniejsze rozmiary? – Do you have it in a smaller size?

Czy macie tę rzecz również w kolorze czarnym? – Do you have it in black?

Z jakiego materiału są te buty? – What fabric are these shoes made of?

Czy mogę dostać większy rozmiar tych butów? – Can I have a bigger size of these shoes?

Ile kosztują te spodnie? – How much do these trousers cost?

Time for a quick revision! Memorize all the Polish phrases once and for all. Try to guess the meaning while going through the phrases.

Dzień dobry, czy mogę to przymierzyć?

Przepraszam, gdzie jest przymierzalnia?

Chciałbym/chciałabym przymierzyć te buty.

Chciałbym/chciałabym zobaczyć tę bluzkę z wystawy.

Noszę rozmiar 36.

Czy mógłby Pan/mogłaby Pani pomóc mi zapiąć ten zamek?

Może to Pan/Pani zapakować to jako prezent?

Czy są większe rozmiary?

Czy są mniejsze rozmiary?

Czy macie tę rzecz również w kolorze czarnym?

Z jakiego materiału są te buty?

Czy mogę dostać większy rozmiar tych butów?

Ile kosztują te spodnie?

Exercise: Say the phrases in Polish.

Ask the shop assistant whether you can try something on.

Ask the shop assistant where the fitting room is.

Ask the shop assistant whether there are bigger sizes.

Ask the shop assistant whether there are smaller sizes.

Ask the shop assistant whether there are different colors.

Ask the shop assistant what fabric the shoes are made of.

Ask the shop assistant how much the shoes cost.

Ask the shop assistant whether he/she can wrap something as a gift.

Ask for help with the zip.

Say what size you wear.

Excellent! You have just bought some nice clothes!

Sightseeing

You have already become fluent in Polish. Think for a moment about the things that you've already acquired. You can introduce yourself, handle a casual conversation, order a meal in a restaurant, and much more. In this part, you will focus on sightseeing and guided tours since you will probably want to visit some interesting places in Poland. Here are a few phrases that may be helpful when sightseeing in Poland.

Dzień dobry, chciałbym/chciałabym wziąć udział w tej wycieczce. – Hello, I would like to take part in this trip.

Czy mógłby Pan/mogłaby Pani polecić mi ciekawe miejsca do zobaczenia? – Could you recommend me some places to visit here?

Czy mógłby Pan/mogłaby Pani polecić mi ciekawe miejsca, które można zwiedzić za darmo? – Could you recommend me some places that are for free?

Czy mogę tutaj robić zdjęcia? – Can I take pictures here?

Co warto tutaj zobaczyć? – What places are worth seeing here?

Jakie restauracje Pani/Pan poleca? – What restaurants do you recommend?

Czy ta wycieczka wymaga dużo chodzenia? – Does this trip require a lot of walking?

Czy mógłby Pan/mogłaby Pani pokazać to na mapie? – Could you show me this on the map?

Co muszę zabrać ze sobą? – What do I need to take with me?

Ile mamy wolnego czasu? – How much free time do we have?

Czy tutaj płaci się za wstęp? – Is there an entrance fee here?

Czy ta wycieczka jest z przewodnikiem? – Is that a guided tour?

Wycieczka była świetna, dziękuję! – The trip was awesome, thank you!

Now repeat the phrases without the English translations.

Dzień dobry, chciałbym/chciałabym wziąć udział w tej wycieczce.

Czy mógłby Pan/mogłaby Pani polecić mi ciekawe miejsca do zobaczenia?

Czy mógłby Pan/mogłaby Pani polecić mi ciekawe miejsca, które można zwiedzić za darmo?

Czy mogę tutaj robić zdjęcia?

Co warto tutaj zobaczyć?

Jakie restauracje Pani/Pan poleca?

Czy ta wycieczka wymaga dużo chodzenia?

Czy mógłby Pan/mogłaby Pani pokazać to na mapie?

Co muszę zabrać ze sobą?

Ile mamy wolnego czasu?

Czy tutaj płaci się za wstęp?

Czy ta wycieczka jest z przewodnikiem?

Wycieczka była świetna, dziękuję!

Exercise: Say the phrases in Polish.

Say that you'd like to take part in a trip.

Ask someone to recommend an interesting place to visit.

Ask someone to recommend a nice restaurant.

Ask the guide whether you can take pictures.

Ask a stranger to show you a place on your map.

Ask how much free time you have.

Ask the travel agency worker whether a trip is with a guide.

Say that the trip was awesome.

Ask whether there is an entrance fee.

Very nice! You can go on a guided trip without any problems. Your Polish is good enough!

Money

Money is one of the most important ingredients for a trip to a foreign country, especially if you need to exchange the currency. Although Poland is a member of the European Union, the country has its own currency—Polish zloty. You can exchange the currency in an exchange office or on the Internet. Nearly all Polish shops and restaurants offer the opportunity of paying with a credit card, so you don't have to worry. Even if you forget about exchanging the money, you can pay with a bank card. If you decide to go to an exchange office, consider learning these phrases prepared for you. They will help you avoid any misunderstanding.

AT THE EXCHANGE OFFICE:

Dzień dobry, chciałbym/chciałabym wymienić moje pieniądze. – Hello, I would like to exchange my money.

Dzień dobry, jaki jest kurs dolara? – What is the US dollar's exchange rate?

Przepraszam, gdzie znajdę kantor wymiany walut? – Excuse me, where can I find the exchange office?

Dzień dobry, chciałbym wymienić moje dolary na złote. – Hello, I would like to exchange my dollars to Polish zloty.

Chciałbym/chciałabym wymienić 500 dolarów. – I would like to exchange 500 US dollars.

Dzień dobry, czy mogę tutaj wymienić kryptowaluty? – Hello, can I exchange cryptocurrencies here?

Repeat all those expressions.

Dzień dobry, chciałbym/chciałabym wymienić moje pieniądze.

Dzień dobry, jaki jest kurs dolara?

Przepraszam, gdzie znajdę kantor wymiany walut?

Dzień dobry, chciałbym wymienić moje dolary na złote.

Chciałbym/chciałabym wymienić 500 dolarów.

Dzień dobry, czy mogę tutaj wymienić kryptowaluty?

Exercise: Try to say the phrases in Polish.

Say that you would like to exchange your money.

Ask about the dollar exchange rate.

Ask a person where the exchange office is.

Say that you would like to exchange 500 US dollars.

Ask whether you can exchange cryptocurrency.

Good job! Money is no longer a problem for you!

AT THE BANK:

There are many different banks in Polish cities, so you will definitely find one very quickly. Moreover, there are many ATMs since Polish people love using bank cards. There is only one big difference—credit cards are very unpopular in Poland. Instead, Polish people use debit cards. The following expressions might be useful at the bank.

Dzień dobry, chciałbym/chciałbym otworzyć konto bankowe. – Hello, I would like to open a new bank account.

Dzień dobry, chciałbym/chciałabym wpłacić pieniądze na moje konto. – Hello, I would like to deposit some cash.

Dzień dobry chciałbym/chciałabym wypłacić pieniądze z mojego konta. – Hello, I would like to withraw some cash from my account.

Przepraszam, gdzie jest najbliższy bankomat? – Excuse me, where is the nearest ATM?

Dzień dobry, mam problem z moją kartą bankową. – Hello, I have a problem with my payment card.

Bankomat nie akceptuje mojej karty. – The ATM doesn't accept my card.

Bankomat połknął moją kartę. – The ATM swallowed my card.

Bankomat nie chce wydać mi gotówki. – The ATM doesn't want to withdraw my money.

Dzień dobry, chciałbym/chciałaby otworzyć konto oszczędnościowe. – Hello, I would like to open a savings account.

Repeat all the expressions now.

Dzień dobry, chciałbym/chciałbym otworzyć konto bankowe.

Dzień dobry, chciałbym/chciałabym wpłacić pieniądze na moje konto.

Dzień dobry chciałbym/chciałabym wypłacić pieniądze z mojego konta.

Przepraszam, gdzie jest najbliższy bankomat?

Dzień dobry, mam problem z moją kartą bankową.

Bankomat nie akceptuje mojej karty.

Bankomat połknął moją kartę.

Bankomat nie chce wydać mi gotówki.

Dzień dobry, chciałbym/chciałaby otworzyć konto oszczędnościowe.

Exercise: Try to say the phrases in Polish.

Tell the bank clerk that you would like to open a bank account.

Tell the bank clerk that you would like to deposit some cash.

Tell the bank clerk that you would like to withdraw some money.

Ask a person where the nearest ATM is.

Tell the bank clerk that you have a problem with your bank card.

Tell the bank clerk that the ATM doesn't accept your card.

Tell the bank clerk that the ATM swallowed your card.

Tell the bank clerk that the ATM doesn't want to withdraw your money.

Tell the bank clerk that you would like to open a savings account.

Good job! You are becoming more and more fluent!

In case of an emergency...

Polish doctors may not know English very well so you should know some basic phrases. In the last chapter of this book, you will find some useful vocabulary (e.g., conditions, medications). Here, though, you will learn how to handle a conversation with a doctor. You will also learn some phrases connected to medical advice in order to understand a Polish doctor.

Boli mnie głowa. – I have a headache.

Boli mnie brzuch. – I have a stomachache.

Mam wysoką gorączkę. – I have a high temperature.

Choruję na cukrzycę. – I have diabetes.

Boli mnie. – I am in pain.

Jestem uczulony/uczulona na laktozę. – I am allergic to lactose.

Jestem przeziębiony/przeziębiona. – I have a cold.

Mam kaszel i katar. – I have a runny nose and a terrible cough.

Złamałem/złamałam nogę. – I have broken my leg.

Złamałem/złamałam rękę. – I have broken my arm.

Skręciłem/skręciłam kostkę. – I have twisted my ankle.

Miałem/miałam wypadek. – I have had an accident.

Chyba mam grypę. – I think I have the flu.

Mam wysokie ciśnienie. – I have high blood pressure.

Wymiotowałem/wymiotowałam cały dzień. – I have been vomiting all day long.

Mam biegunkę. – I have diarrhea.

Kręci mi się w głowie. – I feel dizzy.

Ready for a quick revision? Try to guess the meanings while going through the expressions.

Boli mnie głowa.

Boli mnie brzuch.

Mam wysoką gorączkę.

Choruję na cukrzycę.

Boli mnie.

Jestem uczulony/uczulona na laktozę.

Jestem przeziębiony/przeziębiona.

Mam kaszel i katar.

Złamałem/złamałam nogę.

Złamałem/złamałam rękę.

Skręciłem/skręciłam kostkę.

Miałem/miałam wypadek.

Chyba mam grypę.

Mam wysokie ciśnienie.

Wymiotowałem/wymiotowałam cały dzień.

Mam biegunkę.

Kręci mi się w głowie.

Very good! Now pretend that you are in a doctor's office, and you need to say what is wrong.

Exercise: Try to say the phrases in Polish.

Say to your doctor that you have a headache.

Say to your doctor that you have a stomachache.

Say to your doctor that you have a temperature.

Say to your doctor that you have a cough and runny nose.

Say to your doctor that you have a cold.

Say to your doctor that you have a broken leg.

Say to your doctor that you have a broken arm.

Say to your doctor that you had an accident.

Say to your doctor that you probably have the flu.

Say to your doctor that you feel dizzy.

Say to your doctor that you have diarrhea.

Say to your doctor that you have diabetes.

Very good! You have explained what is wrong. You need to be examined by your doctor right now. Here are some important phrases.

Co Panu/Pani dolega? – What's the matter?

Czy ma Pan/Pani ubezpieczenie? – Do you have health insurance?

Czy bierze Pan/Pani jakieś leki? – Are you on any medication?

Czy pali Pan/Pani papierosy? – Do you smoke cigarettes?

Czy może Pan/Pani opisać objawy? – Could you describe the symptoms?

Od jak dawna ma Pan/Pani te objawy? – How long have you had these symptoms?

Zmierzę Panu/Pani temperature. – I am going to check your temperature.

Proszę się rozebrać/Proszę zdjąć ubranie. – Take your clothes off, please.

Proszę otworzyć usta. – Open your mouth, please.

Musi Pan/pani zostać w łóżku. – You have to stay in bed.

Operacja jest jedyną opcją. – The operation seems to be the only option.

Musi Pan/pani zostać w szpitalu. – You need to stay in hospital.

Oto recepta. – Here's your prescription.

Proszę brać ten lek dwa razy dziennie. – You need to take this medicine twice a day.

Wyniki testu są pozytywne. – The results of the test are positive.

Muszę przepisać antybiotyk. – I need to prescribe an antibiotic.

Repeat these phrases. You need to memorize them.

Co Panu/Pani dolega?

Czy ma Pan/Pani ubezpieczenie?

Czy bierze Pan/Pani jakieś leki?

Czy pali Pan/Pani papierosy?

Czy może Pan/Pani opisać objawy?

Od jak dawna ma Pan/Pani te objawy?

Zmierzę Panu/Pani temperature.

Proszę się rozebrać/Proszę zdjąć ubranie.

Proszę otworzyć usta

Musi Pan/pani zostać w łóżku.

Operacja jest jedyną opcją.

Musi Pan/pani zostać w szpitalu.

Oto recepta.

Proszę brać ten lek dwa razy dziennie.

Muszę przepisać antybiotyk.

At school

Maybe you are a new student and need some help? Maybe you have just taken part in the student exchange program and the first day at Polish school is coming? Don't worry. Below are some useful phrases and questions that will give you confidence. As long as you learn them, you won't get lost at Polish school.

Otwórzcie podręczniki na stronie 46. – Please, open your books on page 46.

Przepraszam, czy mogę wyjść do toalety? – Excuse me, can I go to the toilet?

Czy mógłbyś wytrzeć tablicę? – Could you clean the blackboard, please?

Czy mógłbyś to przeliterować? – Could you spell it out?

Przepraszam, gdzie jest stołówka? – Excuse me, where is the school canteen?

Przepraszam, jak dojdę do sali gimnastycznej? – Excuse me, how can I get to the gym?

O której kończy się lekcja? – What time does the lesson end?

Jakie przedmioty mamy dzisiaj? – Which classes do we have today?

O której godzinie odjeżdża autobus szkolny? – What time does the school bus leave?

Autobus szkolny odjeżdża o 15:00, zaraz po ostatniej lekcji. – The school bus leaves at 3:00 PM, right after the last lesson.

Dzisiejsze zajęcia są odwołane. – Today's classes have been canceled.

Repeat them one more time.

Otwórzcie podręczniki na stronie 46.

Przepraszam, czy mogę wyjść do toalety?

Czy mógłbyś wytrzeć tablicę?

Czy mógłbyś to przeliterować?

Przepraszam, gdzie jest stołówka?

Przepraszam, jak dojdę do sali gimnastycznej?

O której kończy się lekcja?

Jakie przedmioty mamy dzisiaj?

O której godzinie odjeżdża autobus szkolny?

Autobus szkolny odjeżdża o 15:00, zaraz po ostatniej lekcji.

Dzisiejsze zajęcia są odwołane.

Exercise: Try to say the phrases in Polish.

Ask the teacher whether you can go to the toilet.

Ask your friend whether he/she can clean the blackboard.

Ask your friend whether he/she can spell something out.

Ask your friend where the school canteen is.

Ask your friend where the gym is.

Ask your friend what time the lesson ends.

Ask your friend what lessons you have today.

Ask your friend what time the school bus leaves today.

Say to your friend that the lessons have been canceled.

Excellent! With those phrases, you will definitely survive your first day at Polish school. If you would like to learn more words connected to the topic of school, go to the last chapter.

At the university

Being a new student in a foreign country may be overwhelming, especially at the very beginning. You need to get familiar with the building, the city, the culture, and, most importantly, the language. To avoid getting lost on your very first day, go through the expressions below. They won't cover every situation that might happen at your new university, but they will give you the necessary foundations.

Przepraszam, gdzie znajduje się dziekanat? – Excuse me, where is the Dean's office?

Dziekanat znajduje się na trzecim piętrze. – The Dean's office is on the third floor.

Dzisiejsze wykłady są odwołane. – All of today's lectures have been canceled.

Ten wykład jest nieobowiązkowy. – This lecture is non-mandatory.

Przepraszam, o której rozpoczyna się ostatni wykład? – Excuse me, what time does the last lecture start?

Ostatni wykład zaczyna się o 17:00. – The last lecture starts at 5:00 PM.

Dzień dobry, chciałbym/chciałabym wypożyczyć książkę. – Hello, I would like to borrow a book.

Czy mogę zobaczyć Pana/Pani legitymację studencką? – May I see your student ID card?

Dzień dobry, chciałbym/chciałabym wziąć udział w wymianie studenckiej. – Hello, I would like to take part in a student exchange program.

Jestem zainteresowany/zainteresowana studiowaniem w Polsce. – I am interested in studying in Poland.

Repeat the phrases.

Przepraszam, gdzie znajduje się dziekanat?

Dziekanat znajduje się na trzecim piętrze.

Dzisiejsze wykłady są odwołane.

Ten wykład jest nieobowiązkowy.

Przepraszam, o której rozpoczyna się ostatni wykład?

Ostatni wykład zaczyna się o 17:00.

Dzień dobry, chciałbym/chciałabym wypożyczyć książkę.

Czy mogę zobaczyć Pana/Pani legitymację studencką?

Dzień dobry, chciałbym/chciałabym wziąć udział w wymianie studenckiej.

Jestem zainteresowany/zainteresowana studiowaniem w Polsce.

Exercise: Say the phrases in Polish.

Ask your friend where the Dean's office is

Say to your friend where the Dean's office is.

Say that the lectures have been canceled.

Say that the lecture is non-obligatory.

Ask your friend what time the last lecture starts.

Say that the last lecture starts at 5 PM.

Say to the librarian that you would like to borrow a book.

Very nice! If you are considering studying in Poland, don't hesitate. The universities are student-friendly, and the cities are beautiful! If you would like to learn some more vocabulary connected to the topic of university and study, go to the glossary in the last chapter.

At work

A job is one of the main reasons why people decide to move to a foreign country. Starting a new job is a stressful experience, especially at the beginning, since you need to meet your new coworkers and your boss. Moreover, you need to adjust to the new routine and environment. Being a foreigner and not knowing the native language makes the whole situation even worse. The following are some basic expressions that might help you during your first days at a Polish workplace.

Przepraszam, gdzie jest dział kadr? – Excuse me, where is the personnel department?

Proszę przesłać CV oraz podanie o pracę. – Please, send your CV and a job application form.

Pracuję na pół etatu. – I have a part-time job.

Gdzie pracujesz? – Where do you work?

Pracuję w dużej firmie. – I work in a big company.

Co robisz zawodowo? – What do you do professionally?

Jestem prawnikiem. – I am a lawyer.

Gdzie znajduje się firma w której pracujesz? – Where is the company you work at located?

Firma znajduje się w Warszawie. – The company headquarters is located in Warsaw.

Pracuję w systemie zmianowym. – I have a shift job.

O której godzinie kończysz pracę? – What time do you finish your work?

Dziś kończę o 17:00. – Today I'm finishing at 5:00 PM.

Dziś idę na nockę. – Today I'm working a night shift.

Jakie wykształcenie Pan/Pani posiada? – What educational background do you have?

Ukończyłem/ukończyłam uniwersytet. – I graduated/graduated university.

Jakie umiejętności Pan/Pani posiada? – What skills do you have?

Czy posiada Pan/Pani prawo jazdy? – Do you have a driving license?

Tak, posiadam prawo jazdy. – Yes, I have a driving license.

Dostałem/dostałam awans! – I got a promotion.

Czy mogę wziąć dzień wolnego? – Can I take a day off?

Jestem chory/chora. Jutro nie mogę przyjść do pracy. – I am sick. I can't go to work tomorrow.

There were many new expressions, so go through them once again to memorize them.

Przepraszam, gdzie jest dział kadr?

Proszę przesłać CV oraz podanie o pracę.

Pracuję na pół etatu.

Gdzie pracujesz?

Pracuję w dużej firmie.

Co robisz zawodowo?

Jestem prawnikiem.

Gdzie znajduje się firma w której pracujesz?

Firma znajduje się w Warszawie.

Pracuję w systemie zmianowym.

O której godzinie kończysz pracę?

Dziś kończę o 17:00.

Dziś idę na nockę.

Jakie wykształcenie Pan/Pani posiada?

Ukończyłem/ukończyłam uniwersytet.

Jakie umiejętności Pan/Pani posiada?

Czy posiada Pan/Pani prawo jazdy?

Tak, posiadam prawo jazdy.

Dostałem/dostałam awans!

Czy mogę wziąć dzień wolnego?

Jestem chory/chora. Jutro nie mogę przyjść do pracy.

Exercise: Say the phrases in Polish.

Ask your coworker where the personnel department is.

Say that you work a part-time job.

Ask your friend where he/she works.

Say that you work in a big company.

Ask your friend what he/she does professionally.

Say that you are a lawyer.

Say that you work in Warsaw.

Say that you work a shift job.

Tell your interviewer that you have a driver's license.

Tell your interviewer that you graduated from university.

Say to your coworker that you got a promotion.

Excellent! Surviving the first day at work in Poland won't be that stressful for you.

Chapter 4 – Useful Words

Food and Drink

Pieczywo – bakery

Mięso – meat

Produkty mleczne – dairy products

Owoce – fruits

Warzywa – vegetables

Jajka – eggs

Słodycze – sweets/candy

Napoje – beverages

Alkohol – alcohol

Karma dla kota – cat food

Karma dla psa – dog food

Przyprawy – spices

Mrożonki – frozen food

Dania gotowe – convenience food/ready meals

Lody – ice cream

Dairy Products – produkty mleczne:

Mleko – milk

Śmietana – cream

Ser żółty – cheese

Twarożek – cottage cheese

Jogurt – yogurt

Masło – butter

Margaryna – margarine

Maślanka – buttermilk

Bakery – pieczywo:

Chleb – bread

Chleb pszenny – wheat bread

Świeży chleb – fresh bread

Chleb żytni – rye bread

Chleb tostowy – toast bread

Bułka – bread roll

Bagietka – baguette

Pączki – doughnuts

Ciastka – biscuits/cookies

Vegetables – warzywa:

Ziemniak – potato

Pomidor – tomato

Ogórek – cucumber

Papryka czerwona – red pepper

Cebula – onion

Kapusta – cabbage

Sałata – lettuce

Marchewka – carrot

Brokuł – broccoli

Kalafior – cauliflower

Fasola – beans

Czosnek – garlic

Dynia – pumpkin

Szpinak – spinach

Pietruszka – parsley

Soja – soy

Seler – celery

Jarmuż – kale

Burak – beet/beetroot

Batat – sweet potato

Fruits – owoce:

Banan – banana

Jabłko – apple

Pomarańcza – orange

Grejfrut – grapefruit

Cytryna – lemon

Gruszka – pear

Brzoskwinia – peach

Kokos – coconut

Ananas – pineapple

Śliwka – plum

Arbuz – watermelon

Truskawka – strawberry

Malina – raspberry

Jagoda – blueberry

Wiśnia – cherry

Awokado – avocado

Orzech włoski – a walnut

Meat – mięso:

Kiełbasa – sausage

Bekon – bacon

Kurczak – chicken

Drób – poultry

Wołowina – beef

Wieprzowina – pork

Baranina – lamb

Szynka – ham

Mięso mielone – minced meat

Kabanos – a kabanos sausage (a snack stick sausage)

Salami – salami

Sweets/Candy – słodycze:

Czekolada – chocolate

Ciastka – cookies/biscuits

Cukierki czekoladowe – bonbons

Delicje – jaffa cakes

Batonik – chocolate bar

Żelki – jelly beans/gummy bears

Deser – dessert

Galaretka – jelly

Wafelek – wafer

Lody – ice cream

Lizak – lollipop

Krówka – fudge

Landrynki – hard candy

Beverages – napoje:

Woda w butelce – bottled water

Woda mineralna – mineral water

Woda gazowana – sparkling water

Cola – cola

Napoje gazowane – fizzy drinks

Sok pomarańczowy – orange juice

Sok jabłkowy – apple juice

Koktajl owocowy – fruit cocktail/smoothie

Kawa – coffee

Kawa rozpuszczalna – instant coffee

Kawa czarna – black coffee

Kawa z mlekiem – white coffee

Herbata – tea

Gorąca czekolada – hot chocolate

Piwo – beer

Wódka – vodka

Czerwone wino – red wine

Białe wino – white wine

Whisky – whiskey

Other Groceries:

Jajka – eggs

Mąka – flour

Sól – salt

Pieprz – pepper

Cukier – sugar

Cukier brązowy – cane sugar

Ryż – rice

Olej – oil

Oliwa z oliwek – olive oil

Przyprawy – spices

Miód – honey

Płatki kukurydziane – corn flakes

Płatki śniadaniowe – cereal

Healthy/Vegan Products:

Mleko sojowe – soy milk

Jogurt sojowy/kokosowy – soy/coconut yogurt

Mleko ryżowe/migdałowe – Rice/almond milk

Tofu – tofu

Hummus – hummus

Bezglutenowy – gluten-free

Soczewica – lentils

Płatki owsiane – oat flakes

Orzechy – nuts

Nasiona – seeds

Food and Drink – Vocabulary Revision

fruits

ice cream

milk

cheese

yogurt

bread

potato

tomato

red pepper

onion

carrot

broccoli

sweet potato

banana

apple

orange

lemon

watermelon

strawberry

cherry

sausage

bacon

chicken

poultry

ham

chocolate

cookies/biscuits

chocolate bar

dessert

ice cream

bottled water

mineral water

sparkling water

orange juice

apple juice

coffee

black coffee

white coffee

tea

cereal

gluten-free

Colors and Patterns

Kolory – colors

Biały – white

Czarny – black

Niebieski – blue

Granatowy – navy

Szary – gray

Czerwony – red

Zielony – green

Żółty – yellow

Pomarańczowy – orange

Fioletowy – violet/purple

Różowy – pink

Brązowy – brown

Beżowy – beige

Kremowy – creamy

Złoty – gold

Srebrny – silver

Kolorowy – colorful

Bezbarwny – colorless

Przeźroczysty – transparent

Wzory – Patterns:

W paski/pasiasty – striped

W kratę – checkered

W kwiaty – floral

W kropki/w grochy/w groszki – spotted/dotted

Cekinowy – sequin

Koronkowy – lacy/lacey

Lśniący/świecący – shiny

Brokatowy/błyszczący – glittery

Matowy – matt/dull

Colors and Patterns – Vocabulary Revision

white

black

blue

gray

red

green

orange

violet/purple

pink

brown

beige

gold

silver

colorful

striped

floral

spotted/dotted

shiny

Family and Relationships

Family Members

Członkowie rodziny – family members

Rodzina – family

Bliska rodzina – nuclear family

Rodzice – parents

Rodzeństwo – siblings

Dzieci – children

Syn – son

Córka – daughter

Matka – mother (mama – mom)

Ojciec – father (tata – dad)

Ojczym – stepfather

Macocha – stepmother

Brat – brother

Brat przyrodni – stepbrother

Siostra – sister

Siostra przybrana – stepsister

Dziadkowie – grandparents

Babcia – grandmother/grandma

Dziadek – granddad/grandpa

Wnuk – grandson

Wnuczka – granddaughter

Ciocia – aunt

Wujek– uncle

Bratanek/siostrzeniec – nephew

Bratanica/siostrzenica – niece

Kuzyn/kuzynka – cousin

Teść – father-in-law

Teściowa – mother-in-law

Szwagier – brother-in-law

Szwagierka – sister-in-law

Relationships

Pokrewieństwo/relacja – relationship

W związku – in a relationship

Wyśjć za kogoś – to marry somebody

Żonaty (masculine) – zamężna (feminine) – married

Wziąć ślub – to get married

Ślub – wedding

Małżonkowie/małżeństwo – married couple

Mąż – husband

Żona – wife

Pan młody – groom

Panna młoda – bride

Państwo młodzi – bridal couple

Zaręczyć się – to get engaged

Oświadczyć się komuś – to propose to somebody

Zaręczyny – engagement

Pierścionek zaręczynowy – engagement ring

Narzeczony – fiancé

Narzeczona – **fiancée**

Chłopak – boyfriend

Dziewczyna – girlfriend

Chodzić z kimś – to go out with somebody

Randka – date

Randkować – to date

Zerwać z kimś – to break up with somebody

Rozwieść się – to get divorced/to get a divorce

Rozwiedziony/rozwiedziona – divorced

W stanie wolnym/singiel (m.)/singielka (f.) – single

Bezdzietny/bezdzietna – childless

Mieć dzieci – to have children

W ciąży – pregnant

Być w ciąży – to be pregnant

Family and Relationships – Vocabulary Revision

family members

family

parents

siblings

children

son

daughter

mother

father

stepfather

stepmother

brother

sister

grandparents

grandmother/grandma

granddad/grandpa

aunt

uncle

cousin

relationship

to marry somebody

married

to get married

wedding

husband

wife

to get engaged

fiancé

fiancée

boyfriend

girlfriend

date

to break up with somebody

to get divorced/to get a divorce

divorced

single

to have children

to be pregnant

Weather

Prognoza pogody – weather forecast

Pogoda – weather

Słońce – sun

Temperatura – temperature

Świecić – shine

Słonecznie – sunny

Ciepło/ciepły – warm/hot

Zimno/zimny – cold

Chmura – cloud (chmury – clouds)

Zachmurzenie – cloudiness/overcast

Lekkie zachmurzenie – light overcast

Deszcz – rain

Padać – to rain

Przelotne opady – shower

Śnieg – snow

Opady deszczu – rainfall

Intensywne opady deszczu – heavy rainfall

Opady sniegu – snowfall

Intensywne opady śniegu – heavy snowfall

Grad – hail

Mgła – fog

Mglisty/mglisto – foggy

Ograniczona widoczność – limited visibility

Śliska nawierzchnia – slippery road

Ciśnienie atmosferyczne – air pressure

Wilgotność powietrza – air humidity

Niskie ciśnienie – low pressure

Wyskie ciśnienie – high pressure

Burza – storm

Błyskawica – lightning

Grzmot – thunder

Wiatr – wind

Porywy wiatru – wind blasts

Prędkość wiatru – wind speed

Silny wiatr – high wind/strong wind

Burza z piorunami – electrical storm

Wichura – windstorm

Nadciąga wichura – a windstorm is blowing up

Huragan – hurricane

Tornado – tornado

Pówódź/zalanie – flooding

Susza – drought

Przymrozek – freeze

Szron – frost

Szadź – hard rime frost

Weather – Vocabulary Revision

weather

sun

temperature

sunny

warm/hot

cold

cloudiness/overcast

rain

snow

rainfall

hail

fog

slippery road

storm

lightning

thunder

wind

wind speed

windstorm

hurricane

Clothes

Basic Pieces of Clothing:

Bluzka z krótkim rękawem/T-shirt – T-shirt

Koszula – shirt

Bluzka – blouse

Sweter – sweater

Bluza – sweatshirt

Podkoszulek – undershirt

Kurtka/marynarka/żakiet – jacket

Płaszcz – coat

Kamizelka – waistcoat

Garnitur – suit

Spodnie – trousers

Dżinsy/Jeansy – jeans

Spódniczka – skirt

Sukienka – dress

Sukienka mini – mini dress

Sukienka midi – midi dress

Długa sukienka/suknia – long dress

Bielizna – Underwear:

Majtki – pants

Stanik/biustonosz – bra

Skarpetki – socks

Bokserki – boxershorts

Rajstopy – tights

Podkolanówki – tube socks/knee-socks

Kalesony – underdrawers

Odzież zimowa – Winter Clothes:

Szal – scarf

Rękawiczki – gloves

Czapka zimowa – winter hat

Komin – infinity scarf

Kurtka zimowa – winter jacket

Kominiarka narciarska – ski mask

Gogle narciarskie – ski goggles

Spodnie narciarskie – ski pants

Kurtka narciarska – ski jacket

Odzież letnia – Summer Clothes:

Szorty/krótkie spodnie – shorts

Strój kąpielowy – swimsuit

Jednoczęściowy strój kąpielowy – one-piece swimsuit

Dwuczęściowy strój kąpielowy – two-piece swimsuit

Pareo – pareo/pareau (wrap-around skirt)

Kapelusz przeciwsłoneczny – sun hat

Buty – Shoes:

Trampki/Adidasy – gym shoes/sneakers

Sandały – sandals

Kozaki – moon boots/winter shoes

Mokasyny – moccasins

Buty na obcasie – high-heeled shoes/high heels

Buty na koturnie – wedge heels

Półbuty – casual shoes

Buty do wspinaczki – climbing boots

Buty do tańca – dancing shoes

Kapcie – slippers

Klapki/japonki – flip-flops

Balerinki/płaskie buty – flat shoes

Dodatki – Accessories:

Okulary – glasses

Okulary przeciwsłoneczne – sunglasses

Torebka – bag

Torba na zakupy – shopping bag

Czapka z daszkiem – cap

Kapelusz – hat

Pasek – belt

Zegarek – watch

Szelki – braces/suspenders

Krawat – tie

Mucha – bow tie

Portfel – wallet

Kopertówka – clutch bag

Plecak – backpack

Torba na laptopa – laptop bag

Chustka – handkerchief

Biżuteria – Jewelry:

Kolczyki – earrings

Naszynik – necklace

Bransoletka – bracelet/wristband

Bransoletka z wisiorkiem – charm bracelet

Wisiorek – pendant

Broszka – brooch/pin

Spinki do mankietów – links

Kolczyk do nosa – nose ring

Kolczyk na języku – tongue stud

Materiał – Fabric:

Skórzany – leather

Dżinsowy – denim

Sztuczna skóra/skaja – artificial leather

Wełniany – woolen

Bawełniany – cotton

Miękki – soft

Szorstki – coarse

Jedwabny – silken

Satynowy – satin

W sklepie odzieżowym – At the Clothing Store:

Przymierzalnia – fitting room/dressing room

Przymierzać coś – to try something on

Wieszak na ubrania – clothing rack

Kolekcja zimowa/wiosenna – winter/spring collection

Modny – fashionable/trendy

Wystawa – display

Okazja – bargain

Cena okazyjna – bargain price

Karta podarunkowa/karta upominkowa – gift card

Reklamacja – consumer complaint

Zwrot – return

Zwrot pieniędzy – refund

Rozmiar – size

Clothes – Vocabulary Revision

T-shirt

shirt

blouse

sweater

sweatshirt

jacket

coat

suit

trousers

jeans

skirt

dress

pants

bra

socks

scarf

gloves

winter hat

winter jacket

shorts

swimsuit

sun hat

gym shoes/sneakers

sandals

moon boots/winter shoes

high-heeled shoes/high heels

casual shoes

slippers

flip-flops

glasses

sunglasses

bag

shopping bag

cap

hat

belt

watch

tie

wallet

backpack

laptop bag

earrings

necklace

bracelet/wristband

leather

cotton

fitting room/dressing room

clothing rack

fashionable/trendy

bargain

gift card

return

refund

size

Body and Health

Głowa – Head

Twarz – face

Włosy – hair

Uszy – ears (ucho – ear)

Oczy – eyes (oko – eye)

Nos – nose

Usta – mouth

Język – tongue

Zęby – teeth (ząb – tooth)

Szyja – neck

Gardło – throat

Czoło – forehead

Rzęsy – eyelashes (rzęsa – eyelash)

Brwi – eyebrows (brew – eyebrow)

Policzki – cheeks (policzek – cheek)

Górne części ciała – Upper Body

Klatka piersiowa – chest

Plecy – back

Dłoń – hand

Ręka – arm

Łokieć – elbow

Palce – fingers (palec – finger)

Nadgarstek – wrist

Brzuch – stomach

Piersi – breasts

Dolne części ciała – Lower Body

Biodra – hips (biodro – hip)

Pośladki – bottom

Nogi – legs (noga – leg)

Stopy – feet (stopa – foot)

Palce u nóg – toes (palec u nogi – toe)

Kolana – knees (kolano – knee)

Pięty – heels (pięta – heel)

Kostka – ankle

Uda – thighs (udo – thigh)

Łydki – calves (łydka – calf)

Kości i organy wewnętrzne – Bones and Internal Organs

Żebra – ribs (żebro – rib)

Czaszka – skull

Żołądek – stomach

Serce – heart

Płuca – lungs (płuco – lung)

Wątroba – liver

Nerki – kidneys

Naczynia krwionośne – blood vessels

Mięśnie – muscles (mięsień – muscle)

At the Hospital/Health Center:

Szpital – hospital

Ośrodek zdrowia – health center

Poczekalnia – waiting room

Izba przyjęć – casualty department

Szpitalny Oddział Ratunkowy (SOR) – emergency department

Karetka pogotowia/ambulans – ambulance

Karta pacjenta – medical history (chart)

Oddział chirurgiczny – surgical ward

Oddział intensywnej terapii – intensive care unit

Gabinet zabiegowy – doctor's office/treatment room

At the Doctor's Office:

Doktor/lekarz – doctor

Objawy – symptoms (objaw – symptom)

Choroby przewlekłe – chronic diseases

Choroba – disease/illness

Dolegliwość – condition

Zastrzyk – injection

Szczepionka – vaccine

Recepta – prescription

Badanie krwi – a blood test

Badanie USG – ultrasonography/USG

Prześwietlenie/rentgen – X-ray

Mieć prześwietlenie – to have an X-ray

Gips – cast/plaster cast

Ubezpieczenie zdrowotne – health insurance

Ubezpieczony/ubezpieczona – insured

Zwolnienie lekarskie – sick note

Stetoskop – stethoscope

Waga – scale

Igła – needle

Conditions:

Ból głowy – headache

Ból brzucha – stomachache

Ból zęba – toothache

Boleć – to hurt

Ból – ache/pain

Gorączka – fever/temperature

Kaszel – cough

Katar – runny nose

Ból gardła – sore throat

Przeziębienie – cold

Grypa – the flu/influenza

Grypa żołądkowa – gastric flu

Złamana ręka – broken arm

Złamana noga – broken leg

Skręcona kostka – twisted ankle

Spuchnięta kostka – swollen ankle

Siniaki – bruises

Bóle w klatce piersiowej – chest pains

Wymiotować – vomit

Nudności/mdłości – nausea

Biegunka/rozwolnienie – diarrhea

Wysypka – rash

Cukrzyca – diabetes

Uczulony na – allergic to

Ciśnienie krwi – blood pressure

Zatrucie pokarmowe – food poisoning

Medication:

Tabletki na ból głowy – headache tablets

Lekarstwo na przeziębienie – cold remedy

Tabletki przeciw chorobie lokomocyjnej – motion sickness pills

Tabletki nasenne – sleeping pills

Lekarstwo na trawienie – stomach powder/indigestion remedy

Syrop na kaszel – cough syrup

Krople do oczu – eye drops

Krople do nosa – nose drops/nasal drops

Krople żołądkowe – stomach drops

Lek przeciwgorączkowy – antipyretic drug

Bandaż/opatrunek – dressing

Woda utleniona – hydrogen peroxide

Rękawiczki medyczne – medical gloves

Leki antydepresyjne – antidepressants

Leki przeciwgorączkowe – antipyretics

Antybiotyki – antibiotics

Leki uspokajające – tranquilizers

Body and Health – Vocabulary Revision

head

face

hair

ears

eyes

nose

mouth

tongue

teeth

throat

chest

back

hand

arm

fingers

stomach

hips

legs

feet

toes

knees

heels

skull

stomach

heart

lungs

muscles

hospital

health center

waiting room

casualty department

emergency department

ambulance

doctor

disease/illness

condition

injection

vaccine

prescription

health insurance

insured

sick note

headache

stomachache

toothache

fever/temperature

cough

runny nose

sore throat

cold

the flu/influenza

gastric flu

broken arm

broken leg

chest pains

vomit

nausea

diarrhea

diabetes

allergic to

blood pressure

food poisoning

headache tablets

motion sickness pills

sleeping pills

cough syrup

eye drops

stomach drops

dressing

antidepressants

antibiotics

tranquilizers

In the House

Salon/pokój dzienny – living room

Kuchnia – kitchen

Łazienka – bathroom

Sypialnia – bedroom

Strych – attic

Garaż – garage

Dach – roof

Łazienka dla gości – guest bathroom

Ogród – garden

Jadalnia – dining room

Appliances:

Pralka – washing machine

Zmywarka – dishwasher

Mikrofalówka – microwave

Piekarnik – oven

Zlew – sink

Suszarka – hairdryer

Telewizor – TV

Żelazko – iron

Robot kuchenny – food processor

Odkurzacz – vacuum cleaner

Mop – mop

Sokowirówka – juicer

Mikser/blender – blender

Lodówka – fridge

Zamrażarka – freezer

Ładowarka do telefonu – phone charger

In the Kitchen:

Garnek – pot

Patelnia – frying pan

Talerz – plate

Szklanka – glass

Widelec – fork

Nóż – knife

Łyżka – spoon

Łyżeczka – teaspoon

Lada kuchenna – kitchen counter

Kran – tap

Ekspres do kawy – coffee machine

Szafka kuchenna – cupboard

Miska – bowl

Kubek – mug

Filiżanka – teacup/coffee cup

Czynności w domu – Activities at Home:

Sprzątać – to clean

Gotować – to cook

Prasować – to iron

Odkurzać – to vacuum

Myć naczynia – to wash the dishes

Oglądać telewizję – to watch TV

Płacić czynsz – to pay the rent

Myć okna – to clean windows

Odgracać – to declutter

Prać ubrania – to wash the clothes

Podlewać rośliny – to water the plants

Kosić trawnik – to mow the lawn

Myć samochód – to wash the car

Naprawiać – to fix

In the House – Vocabulary Revision

living room

kitchen

bathroom

bedroom

garage

roof

guest bathroom

garden

dining room

washing machine

dishwasher

microwave

oven

sink

hairdryer

TV

iron

vacuum cleaner

fridge

phone charger

pot

frying pan

plate

glass

fork

knife

spoon

teaspoon

tap

coffee machine

cupboard

bowl

mug

teacup/coffee cup

to clean

to cook

to iron

to vacuum

to wash the dishes

to watch TV

to pay the rent

to wash the clothes

to fix

Sport and Fitness

Sports:

Igrzyska Olimpijskie – the Olympic Games

Liga Mistrzów – Champions League

Mecz – match

Piłka nożna – football

Piłka ręczna – handball

Siatkówka – volleyball

Koszykówka – basketball

Baseball – baseball

Futbol amerykański – American football

Skok w dal – long jump

Skok wzwyż – high jump

Skok o tyczce – pole vault

Rzut oszczepem – javelin throw

Rzut młotem – hammer throw

Sprint – sprint

Kolarstwo – cycling

Żużel – speedway

Formuła 1 – Formula One/F1

Tenis – tennis

Badminton – badminton

Golf – golf

Kręgle – bowling

Żeglarstwo – sailing

Tenis stołowy – table tennis

Gimnastyka – gymnastics

Siatkówka plażowa – beach volleyball

Sztuki walki – martial arts

Boks – boxing

Łucznictwo – archery

Strzelanie – shooting

Wyścigi konne – horse racing

Winter Sports:

Jazda na nartach – skiing

Skoki narciarskie – ski jumping

Turniej Czterech Skoczni – Four Hills Tournament

Łyżwiarstwo – ice-skating

Łyżwiarstwo figurowe – figure skating

Łyżwiarstwo szybkie – speed skating

Hokej na lodzie – ice hockey

Jazda na desce – snowboarding

Saneczkarstwo – tobogganing

Bobsleje – bobsleigh

Daily Sport Activities:

Bieganie – running/jogging

Spacer z kijkami/Nordic walking – Nordic walking

Spacerowanie – walking

Jazda na rowerze – bike riding

Jazda na rolkach – rollerblading

Jazda na wrotkach – roller skating

Jazda na deskorolce – skateboarding

Jazda na skuterze wodnym – jetskiing

Jazda na motocyklu – motorcycling

Taniec – dancing

Kalistenika – calisthenics

Wspinaczka górska – climbing

Wspinaczka ściankowa – indoor climbing

Siłownia na powietrzu – outdoor gym

Joga – yoga

Aerobik – aerobics

Aerobik wodny – aquarobics

Pływanie – swimming

Kajakarstwo – canoeing

Extreme Sports:

Skok na bungee – bungee jumping

Skok ze spadochronem – parachute

Spływ górski – white-water rafting

Windsurfing – windsurfing

Szybownictwo – gliding

Nurkowanie pod lodem – ice diving

Alpinizm jaskiniowy – caving

Narciarstwo ekstremalne – extreme skiing

Alpinizm – alpinism

Himalaizm – himalaism

Sports Equipment:

Narty – ski

Deskorolka – skateboard

Rolki – rollerblades

Wrotki – skates

Rower – bike

Łyżwy – skates (for ice-skating)

Motocykl – motorbike

Mata do jogi – yoga mat

Ciężarki – weights

Lina – rope

Kask rowerowy – bicycle helmet

Ochraniacze – athletic support

Strój sportowy – leisurewear

Sanki – sledge

Plecak – backpack

Buty wspinaczkowe – climbing shoes

Buty do biegania – running shoes

Kamizelka ratunkowa – life jacket

Rakieta tenisowa – tennis racket

Rakieta do badmintona – badminton racket

Bolid formuły 1 – Formula 1 car

Spadochron – parachute

Żaglówka – sailing boat

Sport and Fitness – Vocabulary Revision

match

football

handball

volleyball

basketball

baseball

American football

cycling

speedway

tennis

golf

bowling

sailing

beach volleyball

boxing

skiing

ski jumping

ice-skating

snowboarding

running/jogging

Nordic walking

walking

bike riding

rollerblading

roller skating

skateboarding

motorcycling

dancing

climbing

outdoor gym

yoga

aerobics

swimming

bungee jumping

windsurfing

ski

skateboard

rollerblades

skates

bike

skates (for ice-skating)

motorbike

yoga mat

bicycle helmet

athletic support

backpack

climbing shoes

running shoes

life jacket

tennis racket

Countries

Countries – kraje:

Polska – Poland

Wielka Brytania – Great Britain (the UK)

Stany Zjednoczone/USA – United States/USA

Niemcy – Germany

Francja – France

Hiszpania – Spain

Czechy – the Czech Republic

Włochy – Italy

Portugalia – Portugal

Grecja – Grecce

Holandia – the Netherlands

Belgia – Belgium

Węgry – Hungary

Słowacja – Slovakia

Ukraina – Ukraine

Turcja – Turkey

Dania – Denmark

Norwegia – Norway

Szwecja – Sweden

Finlandia – Finland

Chorwacja – Croatia

Irlandia – Ireland

Islandia – Iceland

Rosja – Russia

Chiny – China

Japonia – Japan

Australia – Australia

Brazylia – Brazil

Argentyna – Argentina

Kolumbia – Colombia

Meksyk – Mexico

Kanada – Canada

Egipt – Egypt

Izrael – Israel

Continents – kontynenty:

Ziemia – Earth

Europa – Europe

Azja – Asia

Australia – Australia

Afryka – Africa

Antarktyda – Antarctica

Ameryka Północna – North America

Ameryka Południowa – South America

Ameryka Środkowa – Central America

Countries – Vocabulary Revision

Poland

Great Britain/UK

United States/USA

Germany

France

Spain

the Czech Republic

Italy

Portugal

Grecce

the Netherlands

Belgium

Hungary

Slovakia

Ukraine

Turkey

Denmark

Norway

Sweden

Croatia

Ireland

Iceland

Russia

China

Japan

Australia

Brazil

Argentina

Colombia

Mexico

Canada

Egypt

Israel

Earth

Europe

Asia

Australia

Africa

Antarctica

North America

South America

Central America

Traveling and Holidays

Na lotnisku – At the Airport:

Lotnisko – airport

Samolot – plane

Lot – flight

Bagaż – luggage

Bagaż rejestrowany – hold baggage

Bagaż podręczny – hand baggage

Parking – car park/parking

Strefa wolnocłowa – duty-free zone

Wolny od cła – duty-free

Towary – goods

Toaleta – toilet

Odprawa – check-in

Strażnik/ochroniarz – security guard

Bilet – ticket

Paszport – passport

Kontrola paszportowa – passport control

Dowód osobisty – identity card/ID card

Wejście na pokład – boarding

Lądowanie – landing

Opóźniony – delayed

Odloty – departures

Przyloty – arrivals

Hala odlotów – departure lounge

Lądowanie awaryjne – emergency landing

Międzylądowanie – layover/intermediate landing

Pas bezpieczeństwa – seat belt

Na dworcu autobusowym/kolejowym – At the Train Station/Bus Station:

Dworzec kolejowy – train station/railway station

Dworzec autobusowy – bus station/coach station

Kasa biletowa – ticket office

Pociąg – train

Autobus – bus

Bilet na pociąg/bilet kolejowy – railway ticket

Bilet na autobus/bilet autobusowy – bus ticket

Peron – platform

Tory kolejowe – railway track/railroad track

Kierowca autobusu – bus driver

Konduktor – guard/conductor (the word *konduktor* is only used concerning trains)

Wagon – carriage/car

Przedział – compartment

Wagon sypialny – sleeper/sleeping carriage

Wagon restauracyjny/WARS – diner/restaurant car

Miejsce – seat

Walizka – suitcase

Plecak – backpack

Torebka – purse

Opóźniony – delayed

Przesiadka – change/stopover

Przystanek autobusowy – bus stop

Rozkład jazdy – train schedule/bus schedule

Trasa pociągu – train path

Bilet normalny – full-price ticket

Bilet ulgowy – reduced-fare ticket

Bilet studencki – student ticket

On the Road

Znak drogowy – road sign

Znak ostrzegawczy – warning sign

Znak zakazu – prohibition sigh

Znak nakazu – mandatory sign

Znaki poziome – road surface markings

Ścieżka rowerowa – bike path

Przejście dla pieszych – pedestrian crossing

Lustro drogowe – street mirror

Skrzyżowanie/krzyżówka – intersection/junction

Rondo – roundabout/traffic circle

Wiadukt – flyover

Przejazd kolejowy – railroad crossing/railway crossing

Most – bridge

Parking – parking/car park

Bilet parkingowy – parking ticket

Kwit parkingowy – parking voucher

Zjazd z autostrady – exit ramp

Pas awaryjny – emergency lane

MOP (miejsce obsługi podróżnych) – motorway service area

Tunel – tunnel

Przeprawa promowa – ferry crossing

Limit prędkości – speed limit

Korek – traffic jam

Wypadek samochodowy/wypadek na drodze – car accident

Fotoradar – street camera

Bramki na autostradzie – motorway gates

Paliwo – fuel

Benzyna – petrol/gasoline

Benzyna bezołowiowa – unleaded petrol/lead-free petrol

Benzyna ołowiowa – leaded petrol

Ropa/ON – petroleum

Dystrybutor paliwa – petrol pump/gas pump

Myjnia samochodowa – car wash

Myjnia bezdotykowa – touch-free/touchless car wash

Ulica – street

Droga – road

Sygnalizacja świetlna– traffic lights

Skrzyżowanie – crossroads/junction

Znak drogowy – road sign

Drogowskaz – signpost

Przejście podziemne – underpass

Przejście dla pieszych – pedestrian crossing

Chodnik – pavement/sidewalk

Ścieżka rowerowa – bike path/cycle path

In Your Car:

Pasażer – passenger

Kierowca – driver

Samochód – car

Samochód ciężarowy – lorry/truck

Motocykl – motorbike

Samochód elektryczny – electric car

Kierownica – steering wheel

Siedzenia – seats

Pasy bezpieczeństwa – seat belts

Pedał gazu – accelarator

Hamulec – brake

Hamulec ręczny – handbrake/emergency brake

Skrzynia biegów – gearbox/transmission

Sprzęgło – clutch

Lusterko boczne – wing mirror

Lusterko wsteczne – rearview mirror

Wycieraczki – wipers

Światła do jazdy dziennej/światła krótkie – daytime running lamps

Światła drogowe/światła długie – full beam/driving beam

Światła przeciwmgielne – fog lamps

Kierunkowskaz – indicator/turn signal

Opona – tire

Koło zapasowe – spare wheel

Bagażnik – boot/trunk

Gaśnica – fire extinguisher

Trójkąt ostrzegawczy – warning triangle

Linka holownicza – towrope

Apteczka samochodowa – car emergency kit

Lewarek/podnośnik – jack

Prawo jazdy – driver's license

Dówód rejestracyjny – registration document

Ubezpieczenie OC – liablity insurance

Wypożyczać samochód – rent a car

Wypożyczalnia samochodów – car hire/car rental

Regulamin – rules and regulations

Bak – petrol tank

Olej silnikowy – motor oil

Płyn do spryskiwaczy – windshield washer fluid/screenwash

Silnik – engine/motor

Kinds of Accommodation:

Hotel – hotel

Hostel/schronisko – youth hostel

Pensjonat – pension

Domek/bungalow – bungalow

Kurort/ośrodek wypoczynkowy – resort

Kurort nadmorski – beach resort

Przyczepa kempingowa/kemping – caravan

Obozowisko/pole kempingowe – campsite

Motel – motel

Hotel pięciogwiazdkowy – five-star hotel

Mieszkanie prywatne – private flat

Apartament – suite

Schronisko turystczne – rest house

Schronisko górskie – mountain chalet

Namiot – tent

At a Hotel:

Recepcja – reception

Hol – lobby

Restauracja hotelowa – hotel restaurant

Bar hotelowy – hotel bar

Pokój – room

Klucz – key

Pokój jednoosobowy – single room

Pokój dwuosobowy – double room

Obsługa hotelowa – room service

Parking dla gości – parking space for guests

Piętro/poziom – floor/level

Winda – lift/elevator

Schody – stairs

Balkon – balcony

Taras – terrace/patio

Pokój z aneksem kuchennym – room with a kitchenette

Rezerwować – book/make a reservation

Zameldowanie – check-in

Wymeldowanie – check-out

Pełne wyżywienie – full board

Niepełne wyżywienie – half board

Śniadanie – breakfast

Lunch – lunch

Obiadokolacja – dinner

Przekąski - snacks

In Your Room:

Klimatyzacja – air conditioning

Ogrzewanie – heating

Klucz – key

Łóżko – bed

Łóżko jednoosobowe – twin bed

Łóżko dwuosobowe/łoże małżeńskie – queen bed

Łóżko piętrowe – bunk bed

Garderoba/szafa na ubrania – wardrobe/closet

Stolik nocny – bedside table

Telewizor – TV

Darmowe Wi-Fi – Free Wi-Fi

Hasło do Wi-Fi – Wi-Fi password

Okno – window

Łazienka – bathroom

Wanna – bathtub

Prysznic – shower

Sejf – safe deposit box/safe

Suszarka do włosów – hairdryer

Czajnik bezprzewodowy – electric kettle

Lodówka – fridge

Traveling and Holidays – Vocabulary Revision

an airport

a plane

a flight

luggage

hold baggage

hand baggage

a car park/parking

a toilet

check-in

a security guard

a ticket

a passport

passport control

an identity card/ID card

delayed

departures

arrivals

a departure lounge

a seat belt

a train station/railway station

a bus station/coach station

a ticket office

a train

a bus

a railway ticket

a bus ticket

a platform

a railway track/railroad track

a bus driver

a carriage/car

a compartment

a seat

a suitcase

a backpack

a purse

delayed

a bus stop

a train schedule/bus schedule

a train path

a road sign

a bike path

a pedestrian crossing

an intersection/junction

a roundabout/traffic circle

a bridge

parking/car park

a parking ticket

an exit ramp

an emergency lane

motorway service area

a ferry crossing

speed limit

a traffic jam

a car accident

a street camera

fuel

petrol/gasoline

petroleum

car wash

touch-free/touchless car wash

street

road

traffic lights

a passenger

a driver

a car

a lorry/truck

a motorbike

an electric car

a steering wheel

seats

seat belts

an accelerator

a brake

a handbrake/emergency brake

a gearbox/transmission

wipers

a tire

a spare wheel

a fire extinguisher

a warning triangle

a towrope

a car emergency kit

a jack

a driver's license

a registration document

liability insurance

to rent a car

a car hire/car rental

rules and regulations

a petrol tank

windshield washer fluid/screenwash

an engine/motor

HOLIDAYS:

a hotel

a youth hostel

a pension

a bungalow

a resort

a beach resort

a caravan

a campsite

a motel

a private flat

a suite

a rest house

a mountain chalet

a tent

At a Hotel:

a reception

a lobby

a hotel restaurant

a hotel bar

a room

a key

a single room

a double room

room service

parking space for guests

a floor/a level

a lift/an elevator

stairs

a balcony

a terrace/a patio

a room with a kitchenette

to book/to make a reservation

check-in

check-out

full board

half-board

breakfast

lunch

dinner

In Your Room:

air conditioning

heating

a key

a bed

a twin bed

a queen bed

a bunk bed

a wardrobe/a closet

a bedside table

a TV

Free Wi-Fi

a Wi-Fi password

a window

a bathroom

a bathtub

a shower

a safe deposit box/a safe

a hairdryer

an electric kettle

a fridge

Money

At the Bank:

Bank – bank

Wypłata pieniędzy – cash withdrawal

Wypłacać – withdraw

Gotówka – cash

Karta kredytowa – credit card

Karta zbliżeniowa – tap-and-go card/proximity card

Pieniądze – money

Czek – cheque

Wpłata – deposit

Wpłacać – to deposit

Konto bankowe – bank account

Konto oszczędnościowe – savings account

Oszczędności – savings

Przelew bankowy – bank transfer

Przelew krajowy – domestic transfer

Debet – debit/overdraft

Bankomat – ATM/cash machine

Wpłatomat – CDM/cash deposit machine

Potwierdzenie zapłaty – payment confirmation

Transakcja finansowa – financial transaction

Historia transakcji – transaction history

Kredyt – credit/loan

Kredyt studencki – student loan

Kredyt hipoteczny – mortgage

Kredyt konsumpcyjny – consumer credit

Pożyczka – loan

Dług – debt

Rata – instalment

Odsetki – interest

Lokata – deposit/investment

Stopa procentowa – interest rate

Podatek – tax

Podatek dochodowy – income tax

Podatek VAT – VAT/value-added tax

Faktura – invoice

Umowa – agreement/contract

At the Exchange Office:

Kantor wymiany walut – currency exchange/exchange office

Waluta – currency

Kurs wymiany walut – exchange rate

Bieżący kurs – current rate of exchange

Waluta krajowa – national currency

Wymienić – exchange

Kupić – buy

Sprzedać – sell

Przewalutować – convert a currency

Złoty Polski – Polish zloty

Euro – Euro

Funt brytyjski – British pound

Dolar amerykański – US dollar

Hrywna ukraińska – Ukrainian hryvnia

Korona czeska – Czech koruna

Korona norweska – Norwegian krone

Korona szwedzka – Swedish krone

Forint węgierski – Hungarian forint

Dolar kanadyjski – Canadian dollar

Dolar australijski – Australian dollar

Jen japoński – Japanese yen

Rubel rosyjski – Russian rouble

Rupia indyjska – Indian rupee

Real brazylijski – Brazilian real

Lira turecka – Turkish lira

Kryptowaluta – a cryptocurrency

Bitcoin – Bitcoin

Money – Vocabulary Revision

At the Bank:

bank

cash withdrawal

withdraw

cash

credit card

tap-and-go card/proximity card

money

cheque

deposit

to deposit

bank account

savings account

savings

bank transfer

domestic transfer

debit/overdraft

ATM/cash machine

CDM/cash deposit machine

payment confirmation

financial transaction

transaction history

credit/loan

student loan

mortgage

consumer credit

loan

debt

instalment

interest

deposit/investment

interest rate

tax

income tax

invoice

At the Exchange Office:

currency exchange/exchange office

currency

exchange rate

current rate of exchange

national currency

exchange

buy

sell

convert a currency

Polish zloty

Euro

a cryptocurrency

Bitcoin

School and Education

School Subjects:

Edukacja – education

Język polski – Polish

Matematyka – mathematics/maths

Język obcy – foreign language

Język angielski – English

Język niemiecki – German

Język hiszpański – Spanish

Geografia – geography

Historia – history

Biologia – biology

Chemia – chemistry

Fizyka – physics

Religia – religion

Wychowanie fizyczne (WF) – physical education (PE)

Muzyka – music class

Plastyka – art class

Informatyka – IT class

Godzina wychowawcza – form period/homeroom period

Zajęcia dodatkowe – extracurricular activities

Kółko zainteresowań – special interest group

Zajęcia wyrównawcze – remedial class

Gimnastyka korekcyjna – remedial exercises

Zajęcia praktyczne – practical class

Zajęcia do wyboru – elective courses

Zajęcia wychowawcze – advisory class

Zajęcia wieczorowe – night class

At School:

Nauczyciel – teacher

Uczeń – student

Dyrektor szkoły – school head teacher/school principal

Sala lekcyjna – classroom

Lekcja – lesson

Zajęcia – class

Stołówka – cafeteria/canteen

Sklepik szkolny – tuck shop

Szatnia – changing room

Sala gimnastyczna – school gym

Boisko szkolne – school playground

Sekretariat szkolny – school's secretary office

Biblioteka szkolna – school library

Czytelnia – a reading room

Sala komputerowa – IT suite

Gabinet dyrektora – head teacher's office

Woźny – caretaker

Dzwonek szkolny – school bell

Przerwa – break

Przerwa śniadaniowa – lunch break

Świetlica szkolna – afterschool club

Autobus szkolny – school bus

Wycieczka szkolna – school trip

Sprawdzian/test – test

Ocena – grade (oceny – grades)

Kartkówka – short quiz

Kartkówka ze słówek – vocabulary quiz

Egzamin państwowy – state exam

Uczyć się – to learn/to study

Uczyć się na pamięć – to learn by heart

Czytać – read

Pisać – write

Słuchać – listen

Bawić się/grać – play

Wkuwać – swot/cram

Zaliczyć/zdać test – to pass a test

Oblać test/nie zaliczyć testu – to fail a test

Pisać egzamin – to take a test

Poprawiać test – to retake a test

Egzamin poprawkowy/poprawka – retake

Dziennik lekcyjny – register

Prezentacja – presentation

Egzamin ustny – oral exam

Egzamin pisemny – written exam

Zadanie domowe – homework

Projekt – project

Praca w grupach – group work

Praca w parach – pair work

Rozmowa – conversation

Dyskusja – discussion

Burza mózgów – brainstorm

School Objects:

Podręcznik szkolny – student book

Zeszyt ćwiczeń – workbook

Książka – book

Lektura szkolna – set book

Spis lektur – reading list

Słownik – dictionary

Zeszyt – notebook

Długopis – pen

Ołówek – pencil

Flamaster – marker pen

Kredki – colored pencils

Kredki świecowe – crayons

Farby plakatowe – poster colors/poster paints

Plastelina – plasticine/play dough

Pastele – dry pastels

Pędzel – brush

Blok rysunkowy – sketch pad

Ekierka – set square/triangle

Linijka – ruler

Kątomierz – protractor

Cyrkiel – compass

Gumka do mazania – rubber/eraser

Klej w sztyfcie – glue stick

Nożyczki – scissors

Piórnik – pencil case

Plecak – schoolbag

Ławka szkolna – desk

Tablica – blackboard

Biała tablica – whiteboard

Tablica interaktywna – interactive board

Marker do tablicy – whiteboard marker

Kosz na śmieci – dustbin

Gazetka ścienna – noticeboard/bulletin board

At the University:

Uniwersytet – University/college

Stopień naukowy – degree

Student – student

Wykładowca – lecturer

Wykład – lecture

Sala wykładowa – lecture room

Aula – lecture hall

Licencjat – bachelor's degree

Magister – master's degree

Dyplom/świadectwo – diploma

Zajęcia praktyczne – practicals

Praktykant – trainee

Praktykant w szkole – student teacher

Notatki – notes

Robić notatki – to take notes

Wygłaszać mowę – to give a speech

Przygotowywać prezentację – to prepare a presentation

Badanie – research/study

Przeprowadzać badanie – to conduct research

Wyniki badania – results of the study

Rektor uniwersytetu – college president/university president

Egzamin – exam

Sesja egzaminacyjna – exam session

Zaliczenie warunkowe – conditional promotion

Rok studiów – college level

Praca dyplomowa – thesis

Praca licencjacka – bachelor's thesis/BA thesis

Praca magisterska – master's thesis/MA thesis

Studia zaoczne – extramural studies

Studia dzienne – full-time studies

Kampus uniwersytecki – university campus

Dziekanat – deanery/dean's office

Doktorat – doctorate

Praca doktorancka – Ph.D. thesis

Absolwent – graduate

Absolutorium – graduation ceremony

Wydział – institute

Władze szkoły – school authorities

Rekrutacja – recruitment

Egzaminy wstępne – entrance exams

Wymiana studencka – student exchange program

Indeks – student book

Legtymacja studencka – student ID card

Kredyt studencki – student loan

Akademik – residence hall/dormitory

Europejski System Transferu Punktów (ECTS) – European Credit Transfer System (ECTS)

School and Education – Vocabulary Revision

School Subjects:

education

Polish

mathematics/maths

foreign language

English

German

Spanish

geography

history

biology

chemistry

physics

physical education (PE)

music class

art class

IT class

form period/homeroom period

extracurricular activities

special interest group

remedial class

remedial exercises

practical class

At School:

teacher

student

school head teacher/school principal

classroom

lesson

class

cafeteria/canteen

tuck shop

changing room

school gym

school playground

school's secretary office

school library

a reading room

IT suite

head teacher's office

caretaker

school bell

break

lunch break

afterschool club

school bus

school trip

test

grade

short quiz

vocabulary quiz

state exam

to learn/to study

to learn by heart

read

write

listen

play

swot/cram

to pass a test

to fail a test

to take a test

to retake a test

retake

register

presentation

oral exam

written exam

homework

project

group work

pairwork

conversation

discussion

brainstorm

School Objects:

student book

workbook

book

set book

reading list

dictionary

notebook

pen

pencil

marker pen

colored pencils

crayons

poster colors/poster paints

plasticine/play dough

dry pastels

brush

sketch pad

set square/triangle

ruler

protractor

compass

rubber/eraser

glue stick

scissors

pencil case

schoolbag

desk

blackboard

whiteboard

interactive board

whiteboard marker

dustbin

noticeboard/bulletin board

At the University:

University/college

degree

student

lecturer

lecture room

lecture hall

bachelor's degree

master's degree

diploma

practicals

trainee

student teacher

to take notes

to give a speech

to prepare a presentation

research/study

to conduct research

results of the study

college president/university president

exam

exam session

conditional promotion

college level

thesis

bachelor's thesis/BA thesis

master's thesis/MA thesis

extramural studies

full-time studies

university campus

deanery/dean's office

Ph.D. thesis

graduate

graduation ceremony

institute

school authorities

recruitment

entrance exams

student exchange program

student book

student ID card

student loan

residence hall/dormitory

Work and Career

Professions:

Zawód – profession

Lekarz – doctor

Nauczyciel – teacher

Biznesmen – businessman

Bizneswoman – businesswoman

Prawnik – lawyer

Pielęgniarka – nurse

Sprzedawca – shop assistant

Księgowy/księgowa – accountant

Strażak – firefighter

Żołnież – soldier

Policjant – policeman

Policjantka – policewoman

Szef kuchni – chef

Kucharz – cook

Kelner – waiter

Kelnerka – waitress

Pilot – pilot

Naukowiec – scientist

Listonosz – postman

Tłumacz – translator

Mechanik – mechanic

Hydraulik – plumber

Malarz – painter

Aktor – actor

Aktorka – actress

Kierowca – driver

Sprzątacz/sprzątaczka – cleaner

Dentysta – dentist

Rolnik – farmer

Inżynier – engineer

Kierownik/menedżer – manager

Fotograf – photographer

Muzyk – musician

Sekretarz/sekretarka – secretary

Kierowca taksówki – taxi driver

Pisarz – writer

Opiekun/opiekunka – babysitter

Piekarz – baker

Fryzjer – hairdresser

Filmowiec – filmmaker

Dziennikarz – journalist

Ksiądz – priest

Weterynarz – vet

Psycholog – psychologist

Badacz – researcher

At a Workplace:

Miejsce pracy – workplace

Biuro – office

Praca – job

Fabryka – factory

Firma – company

Siedziba firmy – headquarters

Korporacja – corporation

Pracownik – employee

Pracodawca – employer

Szef/szefowa – boss

Koledzy z pracy – colleagues/coworkers

Praca zdalna – remote working

Pracownik fizyczny – blue-collar worker

Pracować – work

Wypłata – salary

Zarobki – earnings/wages

Brutto – gross

Netto – post-tax

Podatek – tax

Awans – promotion

Dostać awans – to get a promotion

Dostać pracę – to get a job

Być zwolnionym – to be dismissed

Być zwolnionym natychmiastowo – to be fired

Zredukować personel – to make people redundant

Podwyżka – pay rise

Dostać podwyżkę – to get a pay rise

Praca na cały etat – full-time job

Praca na pół etatu – part-time job

Praca dodatkowa – side job

Praca zmianowa – shift job

Nocna zmiana/nocka – night shift

Rozmowa o pracę – job interview

Umowa o pracę – job agreement

Życiorys (CV) – curriculum vitae (CV)

Podanie o pracę – job application form

Stanowisko – position

Kwalifikacje – qualifications

Wymagania – requirements

Umiejętności – skills

Wykształcenie – education

Doświadczenie zawodowe – job experience

Dział kadr – personnel department/HR

Dział obsługi klienta – customer service department

Dział wsparcia technicznego – help desk

Wyjazd służbowy – business trip

Notatka służbowa – memo

Spotkanie – meeting

Urlop – leave

Urlop macierzyński – maternity leave

Urlop zdrowotny – sick leave

Urlop bezpłatny – unpaid leave

Płatny urlop wypoczynkowy – paid vacation leave

Work and Career – Vocabulary Revision

Professions:

profession

doctor

teacher

businessman

businesswoman

lawyer

nurse

shop assistant

accountant

firefighter

soldier

policeman

policewoman

chef

cook

waiter

waitress

pilot

scientist

postman

translator

mechanic

plumber

painter

actor

actress

driver

cleaner

dentist

farmer

engineer

manager

photographer

musician

secretary

taxi driver

writer

babysitter

baker

hairdresser

filmmaker

journalist

priest

vet

psychologist

researcher

At a Workplace:

workplace

office

job

factory

company

headquarters

corporation

employee

employer

boss

colleagues/coworkers

remote working

blue-collar worker

work

salary

earnings/wages

gross

post-tax

tax

promotion

to get a promotion

to get a job

to be dismissed

to be fired

to make people redundant

pay rise

to get a pay rise

full-time job

part-time job

side job

shift job

night shift

job interview

job agreement

curriculum vitae (CV)

application form

position

qualifications

requirements

skills

education

job experience

personnel department/HR

customer service department

help desk

memo

meeting

leave

maternity leave

sick leave

unpaid leave

paid vacation leave

Doing the Shopping

Sklep – shop

Sklep spożywczy – grocery store

Sklep odzieżowy – clothing shop

Skep obuwniczy – shoe shop

Piekarnia – bakery/baker's

Cukiernia – confectionery

Księgarnia – bookshop

Stacja benzynowa – petrol station/gas station

Apteka – pharmacy

Drogeria – drugstore/chemist

Kiosk – paper shop/newsagent's/kiosk

Supermarket – supermarket

Sklep samoobsługowy – self-service shop

Sklep sportowy – sports shop

Sklep monopolowy – liquor store/off-licence

Sklep mięsny – butcher's shop/meat market

Sklep z narzędziami – hardware shop

Sklep wielobranżowy – general store

Sklep z upominkami – gift shop

Sklep z pamiątkami – souvenir shop

Sklep wolnocłowy – duty-free shop

Pieniądze – money

Gotówka – cash

Karta płatnicza – payment card/credit card (In Polish stores, people usually say *karta* [card])

Reszta/drobne – change

Banknot – banknote

Terminal płatniczy – payment terminal

Paragon – receipt

Wózek – shopping cart/shopping basket

Produkt – product

Kasa – checkout

Wyprzedaż – sale

Promocja – special offer

Karta podarunkowa – gift card

Zwrot – return

At the Supermarket:

Wejście – entrance

Wyjście – exit

Kasa – checkout

Kasa samoobsługowa – self-service checkout

Torebka plastikowa – plastic bag

Torba na zakupy – shopping bag

Waga – scales

Alejka – aisle

Artykuły spożywcze – groceries

Artykuły codziennego użytku – convenience goods

Artykuły toaletowe – toiletries

Artykuły biurowe – office supplies/stationery

Podstawowe kosmetyki – Basic Toiletries:

Żel pod prysznic – shower gel

Szampon do włosów – shampoo

Odżywka do włosów – hair conditioner

Dezodorant – deodorant

Mydło – soap

Krem do rąk – hand cream

Balsam do ciała – body lotion

Szczoteczka do zębów – toothbrush

Pasta do zębów – toothpaste

Maszynka do golenia – razor

Płyn po goleniu – aftershave

Pianka do golenia – shaving cream

Papier toaletowy – toilet paper

Chusteczki higieniczne – tissues/wipes

Podpaski – period pads

Tampony – tampons

Lakier do paznokci – nail polish

Zmywacz do paznokci – nail polish remover

Płyn micelarny – micellar water

Płatki kosmetyczne/waciki – cotton pads

Gąbka – sponge

Perfumy – perfume

Produkty do makijażu – Makeup Products:

Podkład – foundation

Cień do powiek – eyeshadow

Kredka do oczu – eye pencil

Eyeliner – eyeliner

Szminka/pomadka – lipstick

Tusz do rzęs/maskara – mascara

Korektor – concealer

Bronzer/róż – bronzer/blush

Produkty do sprzątania – Cleaning Products:

Uniwersalny środek czyszczący – all-purpose cleaner

Proszek do prania – washing powder

Szczoteczka do czyszczenia – cleaning brush

Ściereczka do naczyń – dish towel

Płyn do mycia naczyń – dish soap

Płyn do mycia szyb – window cleaner

Gąbka – sponge

Produkty dla dzieci – Products for Babies

Pieluchy jednorazowe/pampersy – disposable diapers

Smoczek – comforter

Mleko dla niemowląt – baby milk/baby formula

Chusteczki dla niemowląt – baby wipes

Books:

Książka – book

Powieść – novel

Literatura piękna – fiction

Literatura faktu – non-fiction

Literatura dziecięca – children's literature

Przewodnik turystyczny/przewodnik – guidebook

Mapa – map

Plan miasta – a town map – city plan

Bajki dla dzieci – storybooks

Stationery:

Zeszyt/notatnik – notebook

Długopis – pencil

Ołówek – pen

Kredki – colored pencils

Flamaster/pisak – marker pen

Gumka do mazania – rubber/eraser

Temperówka – pencil sharpener

Spinacz do papieru – paper clip

Teczka – file/folder

Taśma klejąca – sticky tape

Souvenirs:

Pamiątki z podróży – souvenirs

Sklep z pamiątkami – souvenir shop

Na pamiątkę – as a souvenir

Koszulka – T-shirt

Kubek – mug

Pocztówka – postcard

Posążek/figurka – figurine

Zapalniczka – lighter

Brelok/breloczek – key fob

Długopis – pen

Magnes na lodówkę – fridge magnet

Zabawka – toy

Książka – book

Etui na okulary – spectacle case

Etui na telefon – phone case

Doing the shopping – Vocabulary Revision

a shop

a grocery store

a clothing shop

a shoe shop

a bakery/baker's

a confectionery

a bookshop

a petrol station/gas station

a pharmacy

a drugstore/chemist

a paper shop/newsagent's/kiosk

a supermarket

a self-service shop

a sports shop

a liquor store/off-licence

a butcher's shop/meat market

a hardware shop

a general store

a gift shop

a souvenir shop

a duty-free shop

money

cash

payment card/credit card

change

a banknote

a payment terminal

a receipt

a shopping cart/shopping basket

a product

a checkout

sale

a special offer

a gift card

a return

At the Supermarket:

entrance

exit

a checkout

a self-service checkout

a plastic bag

a shopping bag

scales

an aisle

groceries

convenience goods

toiletries

office supplies/stationery

Podstawowe kosmetyki – Basic Toiletries:

shower gel

shampoo

hair conditioner

deodorant

soap

hand cream

body lotion

toothbrush

toothpaste

razor

aftershave

shaving cream

toilet paper

tissues/wipes

period pads

tampons

nail polish

nail polish remover

micellar water

cotton pads

sponge

perfume

Produkty do makijażu – Makeup Products:

foundation

eyeshadow

eye pencil

eyeliner

lipstick

mascara

concealer

bronzer/blush

Produkty do sprzątania – Cleaning Products:

all-purpose cleaner

washing powder

cleaning brush

dish towel

dish soap

window cleaner

sponge

Produkty dla dzieci – Products for Babies

disposable diapers

comforter

baby milk/baby formula

baby wipes

Books:

book

novel

fiction

non-fiction

children's literature

guidebook

map

a town map/city plan

storybooks

Stationery:

notebook

pencil

pen

colored pencils

marker pen

rubber/eraser

pencil sharpener

paper clip

file/folder

sticky tape

Souvenirs:

souvenirs

souvenir shop

as a souvenir

T-shirt

mug

postcard

figurine

lighter

key fob

pen

fridge magnet

toy

book

spectacle case

phone case

Sightseeing and Entertainment

Centrum informacji turystycznej – tourist center

Punkt informacji turystycznej – tourist information center

Przewodnik – guide

Przewodnik turystyczny – guidebook

Mapa – map

Plan miasta – city plan

Biuro podróży – travel agency

Rezydent turystyczny – holiday representative

Wycieczka – trip

Wycieczka jednodniowa – day trip

Wycieczka autokarowa – coach trip

Zwiedzanie – tour

Zwiedzanie z przewodnikiem – guided tour

Zwiedzać – to do sightseeing

Wycieczka zorganizowana – organized trip

Zwiedzanie miasta – city tour

Opłata za wstęp – entrance fee

Miejsce zbiórki – assembling point

Czas wolny – free time

Places to Visit in A Town:

Stare miasto – Old town

Kamienice zabytkowe – old tenement buildings

Pomnik – monument

Ratusz – town hall

Ratusz Staromiejski – Old Town Hall

Budynek zabytkowy – heritage building

Pomnik zabytkowy – ancient monument

Budynek sejmu – parliament building

Muzeum – museum

Muzeum nauki – science museum

Muzeum historyczne – history museum

Muzeum narodowe – national museum

Muzeum wojskowe – military and war museum

Muzeum na powietrzu – open-air museum

Galeria sztuki – art gallery

Wystawa – exhibition

Park – park

Most – bridge

Promenada – promenade

Deptak – pedestrian zone/pedestrian street

Kościół – church

Bazylika – basilica

At the cinema:

Kino – cinema

Film – film/movie

Film akcji – action film

Thriller – thriller

Komedia romantyczna – romantic comedy

Komedia – comedy

Horror – horror film

Film historyczny – historical film

Film przygodowy – adventure film

Film science fiction – science-fiction film

Musical/film muzyczny – musical

Sala kinowa – screening room

Miejsce – seat

Rząd – row

Ekran – screen

Bar przekąskowy – snack bar

Popcorn – popcorn

Zimne napoje – cold beverages

Bilet do kina – cinema ticket

At the Theater/Opera:

Teatr – theater

Teatr muzyczny – musical theater

Sztuka – play

Spektakl/przedstawienie – performance

Występować – perform

Aktor/aktorka – actor

Główna rola – lead/major role

Balet – ballet

Balet klasyczny – classical ballet

Kurtyna – curtain

Rekwizyt – prop/stage prop

Scena – stage

Opera – opera

Opera – opera house

Operetka – operetta

Musical – musical

Chór – choir

tancerz/tancerka – dancer

śpiewak operowy – opera singer (masculine)

śpiewaczka operowa – opera singer (feminine)

Nightlife:

Klub nocny/klub – nightclub

Klub muzyczny – music club

Bar/pub – bar/pub

Dyskoteka – disco

Barman – barman/bartender

Barmanka – barmaid/bartender

Parkiet – dance floor

Tańczyć – dance

Muzyka – music

Karaoke – karaoke

Śpiewać – sing

Imprezować – party

Spędzać czas z przyjaciółmi – spend time with friends

Zespół muzyczny – music group

DJ/didżej – DJ/club DJ

Drink/koktajl – cocktail

Loża VIP – VIP lounge

Ochroniarze – security guards

At the Swimming Pool:

Akwapark/aquapark – water park

Pływać – swim

Basen kryty – indoor swimming pool

Basen odkryty – outdoor swimming pool

Ręcznik kąpielowy – bath towel

Kółko do pływania – swim ring

Deska do pływania – swimming board

Pływaczki – armbands

Ratownik – life guard

Strój kąpielowy – swimsuit

Przebieralnia – changing room

Przebieralnia damska – women's changing room

Przebieralnia męska – men's changing room

Sauna – sauna

Uzdrowisko/spa – spa

Ośrodek odnowy biologicznej – health spa

Masaż – massage

Masaż twarzy – face massage

Zabieg – treatment

Jacuzzi – hot tub/Jacuzzi

At the Gym:

Karnet na siłownię – gym membership

Trening – workout

Trening kondycyjny – circuit training

Trening siłowy – strength training

Ćwiczenia – exercises

Z przerwami – intervals

Bieżnia stacjonarna/bieżnia – treadmill

Orbitrek – elliptical trainer/cross-trainer

Rower stacjonarny – exercise bicycle

Przyrząd do ćwiczeń siłowych – weight machine

Trening cardio – cardio workout

Podnoszenie ciężarów – weightlifting

Aerobik – aerobics

Mata do ćwiczeń – workout mat

Brzuszki – sit-ups

Przysiady – squats

Pompki – press-ups/push-ups

Hula hop – hula hoop

Skakanka – skipping rope

Ćwiczenia gimnastyczne – keep fit exercises

Strój na siłownię – gym clothes

Leginssy na siłownię – gym leggings

In the Park:

Spacer – walk

Przechadzka – stroll

Spacerować – walk

Drzewo – tree

Staw – pond

Ławka – bench

Fontanna – fountain

Ścieżka/aleja – alley

Kwiaty – flowers

Liście – leaves

Krzewy – bushes

Krzewy różnane – rose bushes

Oranżeria – hothouse/orangery

Trawnik – lawn/grass

Miejsce piknikowe – picnic area

Kosz na śmieci – waste bin

Plac zabaw – playground

Huśtawka – swing

Karuzela – roundabout/carousel

Zjeżdżalnia – playground slide

Ptaki – birds

Kaczka – duck

Łabędź – swan

Wiewiórka – squirrel

Róża – rose

Dąb – oak tree

Klon – maple tree

Świerk – spruce

Sosna – pine tree

Kasztanowiec – chestnut tree

Żołędzie – acorns

Kasztany – chestnuts

In the Church:

Bazylika – basilica

Kościół katolicki – Catholic church

Parafia – parish

Ławka kościelna – pew

Ołtarza – altar

Ambona – pulpit

Msza święta – church service/mass

Organy – organ

Ksiądz – priest

Zakonnica – nun

Zakonnik – monk

Organista – organist

Rzeźba – sculpture

Ofiara – collection (collecting money)

Prezbiterium – chancel/presbytery

Dzwonnica – bell tower

Kaplica – chapel

Dzwon – bell

Wieża kościelna – church tower

Cmentarz – cemetery/churchyard

Sightseeing and Entertainment – Vocabulary Revision

tourist center

tourist information center

guide

guidebook

map

city plan

travel agency

holiday representative

trip

day trip

coach trip

tour

guided tour

to do sightseeing

organized trip

city tour

entrance fee

assembling point

free time

Places to Visit in A Town:

Old town

old tenement buildings

monument

town hall

Old Town Hall

heritage building

ancient monument

parliament building

museum

science museum

history museum

national museum

open-air museum

art gallery

exhibition

park

bridge

promenade

pedestrian zone/pedestrian street

church

basilica

At the Cinema:

cinema

film/movie

action film

thriller

romantic comedy

comedy

horror film

historical film

science-fiction film

musical

screening room

seat

row

screen

snack bar

popcorn

cold beverages

cinema ticket

At the Theater/Opera:

theater

musical theater

play

performance

perform

actor

lead/major role

ballet

classical ballet

curtain

prop/stage prop

stage

opera

opera house

operetta

musical

choir

dancer

opera singer (masculine)

opera singer (feminine)

Nightlife:

nightclub

music club

bar/pub

disco

barman/bartender

barmaid/bartender

dance floor

dance

music

karaoke

sing

party

spend time with friends

music group

DJ/club DJ

cocktail

VIP lounge

security guards

At the Swimming Pool:

water park

swim

indoor swimming pool

outdoor swimming pool

bath towel

swim ring

swimming board

armbands

lifeguard

swimsuit

changing room

women's changing room

men's changing room

sauna

spa

health spa

massage

face massage

treatment

hot tub/Jacuzzi

At the Gym:

gym membership

workout

circuit training

strength training

exercises

intervals

treadmill

elliptical trainer/cross-trainer

exercise bicycle

weight machine

cardio workout

weightlifting

aerobics

workout mat

sit-ups

squats

press-ups/push-ups

hula hoop

skipping rope

keep fit exercises

gym clothes

gym leggings

In the Park:

walk

stroll

walk

tree

pond

bench

fountain

alley

flowers

leaves

bushes

rose bushes

hothouse/orangery

lawn/grass

picnic area

waste bin

playground

swing

roundabout/carousel

playground slide

birds

duck

swan

squirrel

rose

oak tree

maple tree

spruce

pine

chestnut tree

acorns

chestnuts

In the Church:

basilica

Catholic church

parish

pew

altar

pulpit

church service/mass

organ

priest

nun

monk

organist

sculpture

collection (collecting money)

chancel/presbytery

bell tower

chapel

bell

church tower

cemetery/churchyard